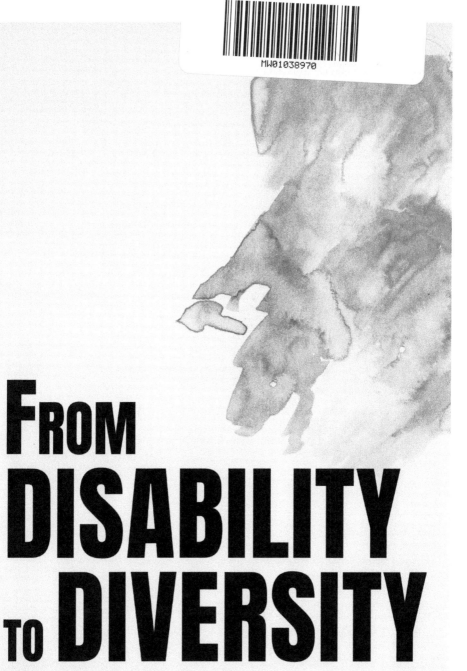

From
DISABILITY
to DIVERSITY

College Success for Students with Learning Disabilities,
ADHD, and Autism Spectrum Disorder

Lynne C. Shea, Linda Hecker, and Adam R. Lalor

Cite as:
Shea, L. C., Hecker, L., & Lalor, A. R. (2019). *From disability to diversity: College success for students with learning disabilities, ADHD, and autism spectrum disorder.* Columbia, SC: University of South Carolina, National Resource Center for The First-Year Experience & Students in Transition.

ISBN: 918-1-942072-29-4
Published by:
National Resource Center for The First-Year Experience® and Students in Transition
University of South Carolina
1728 College Street, Columbia, SC 29208
www.sc.edu/fye

The First-Year Experience® is a service mark of the University of South Carolina. A license may be granted upon written request to use the term "The First-Year Experience." This license is not transferable without written approval of the University of South Carolina.

Production Staff for the National Resource Center:

Project Manager:	Tracy L. Skipper, Assistant Director for Publications
Design and Production:	Andi Breeland, Graphic Artist
	Stephanie L. McFerrin, Graphic Artist
External Reviewers:	Jean M. Henscheid, Idaho State Board of Education
	Ryan Wells, University of Massachusetts Amherst
	Lee Burdette Williams, College Autism Network

Library of Congress Cataloging-in-Publication Data

Names: Shea, Lynne C., author.
  Title: From disability to diversity : college success for students with
    learning disabilities, ADHD, and autism spectrum disorder / Lynne C. Shea,
    Linda Hecker, and Adam R. Lalor.
  Description: Columbia, South Carolina : National Resource Center for The
    First-Year Experience and Students in Transition, University of South
    Carolina, [2019] | Includes bibliographical references and index.
  Identifiers: LCCN 2018036982 (print) | LCCN 2018055971 (ebook) | ISBN
    9781942072300 (Epub) | ISBN 9781942072317 (Ebrary) | ISBN 9781942072294 |
    ISBN 9781942072294? (Paperback)
  Subjects: LCSH: Learning disabled--Education (Higher) | Autistic
    people--Education (Higher) | College students with disabilities--Services
    for.
  Classification: LCC LC4818.38 (ebook) | LCC LC4818.38 .S53 2019 (print) | DDC
    371.92--dc23
  LC record available at https://lccn.loc.gov/2018036982

CONTENTS

TABLES AND FIGURES

Tables

Figures

FOREWORD

Students with learning disabilities, attention-deficit/hyperactivity disorder (ADHD), and autism spectrum disorder (ASD) are often a mystery to faculty and administrators in higher education. As a result, educators are often unprepared to serve this unique but growing group of students. The purpose of this book is to provide useful information for those working in postsecondary contexts who are not yet experts in supporting these students. The acronym *LD* will be used in this book to collectively identify three diagnoses that have implications for learning: learning disabilities, ADHD, and ASD.

The authors all work at Landmark College, an associate- and baccalaureate-granting college in Putney, Vermont, that exclusively serves students with LD. Founded in 1985, the mission of Landmark College is to provide a high-quality education to a variety of students who learn differently. The college has long engaged in research, outreach, and advocacy work to improve K-20 education for all learners. With the creation of the Center for Neurodiversity in 2017, Landmark College recognizes the broad neurodevelopmental variations in learners and embraces a next-generation perspective that is based on both scientific evidence and social justice principles.

At our core, we promote a philosophy of universal design for education (see Chapters 4 and 6), believing that accessibility means moving beyond the accommodations model to create environments that are learner-friendly to as many students as possible. This perspective is essential if we are to take advantage of the strengths and potential contributions of the growing number of individuals with LD who currently attend college.

Although the way Landmark College serves students is unquestionably unique, due to its specialized student population and the high degree of expertise in LD possessed by its faculty and staff, our knowledge of and involvement in the field of disability and higher education is broad and multifaceted, keeping us abreast of research and the concerns of postsecondary personnel nationally and internationally. As part of our work for the Landmark College Institute for Research and Training, we have conducted research individually and in collaboration with colleagues at other postsecondary institutions, published in peer-reviewed journals, organized and presented at international conferences, and provided training and consulting to hundreds of schools, colleges, and universities across the country and across the world. We have served in positions of leadership within national organizations such as the International Dyslexia Association, the Learning Disabilities Association of America, and the Council for Exceptional Children. We have tried to synthesize our broad understanding of issues related to higher education and students with learning disabilities, ADHD, and ASD with our unique Landmark College perspective of pedagogical activism. The results of these efforts are presented in this work.

We could not have done this without the support of the many students, parents, and colleagues at Landmark College and other institutions who generously shared their experiences, insights, and wisdom. We dedicate this book to all those who work to develop educational programs and systems that acknowledge, celebrate, and ensure environments of access and opportunity for diverse learners.

Chapter 1

Introduction: The Postsecondary Context of LD

Students with learning disabilities, attention-deficit/hyperactivity disorder (ADHD), and autism spectrum disorder (ASD) have been pursuing higher education for decades, but their presence has often been overlooked or seen as problematic. Whereas students with physical or sensory disabilities, such as blindness or mobility impairments, are usually viewed as appropriate candidates for higher education, students whose disabilities are associated with learning may encounter questions about whether they even belong in academia. For instance, many falsely believe that if someone's disability relates to learning, by definition they lack the intelligence necessary to obtain a college education. In fact, students with learning disabilities, ADHD, and ASD can be as intelligent as their peers without these disabilities. The challenge associated with higher education for students with learning disabilities, ADHD, and ASD is one that is socially constructed. Essentially, these students have the capacity to learn and develop in college, but the academic and social environments often fail to meet their needs. The barrier to accessing education is not intrinsic to the student but is created by a mismatch between the student and the educational environment. To address these barriers, educators need to rethink how they ensure educational access to all aspects of college and university life. The design, delivery, and assessment of learning and the development of programs, policies, and environments need to be addressed—sometimes at a fundamental level that questions assumptions and beliefs about the nature of education. In spite of these challenges, we argue that students with learning disabilities, ADHD, and ASD not only belong in higher education, they have much to contribute to academic discourse by virtue of unique strengths and perspectives that are part of their cognitive profiles. We also advocate for reframing the concept of learning disabilities, ADHD, and ASD from a traditional medical model that describes learners in terms of individual deficits and disorders to a more socially constructed diversity model that acknowledges the role of both the individual and the environment in understanding what makes learning difficult.

While acknowledging the common use of the term *disability* in research, clinical work, and legal contexts, we prefer the term *learning differences* because of stigma associated with the concept of disability. Traditionally, *learning disability* refers only to specific language-based learning disorders such as dyslexia and dyscalculia. To be clear, ADHD and ASD also have implications for learning but have not been categorized as learning disabilities. Instead, they have traditionally been designated as behavioral or psychiatric disorders. For these reasons, we have chosen to use *students with learning differences* in this book to refer to students with learning disabilities, ADHD, and ASD as a group so as to (a) acknowledge the learning implications associated with diagnoses in any of these areas, (b) highlight that students with these profiles constitute normal variation in learning as opposed to lacking ability to learn, and (c) offer a shorthand throughout the text when referring to these profiles in the aggregate. Moreover, the abbreviation *LD* should be read as *learning differences* rather than *learning disabilities*. When describing research findings or diagnostic characteristics, we will reference the specific profile as appropriate.

Importance of Postsecondary Education for Students with LD

Obtaining a college degree is more important than ever. More than 17 million students in the United States enrolled in postsecondary institutions in 2016, and it is no wonder as to why: The employment prospects for individuals with a college degree are much more favorable than for those without degrees. That year, the employment-to-population ratio for 20- to 24-year-olds was 89% for those with a bachelor's degree or higher, a rate 22% higher than for individuals who completed only high school (67%; McFarland et al., 2017). For individuals with disabilities, employment rates are particularly low, as only 32% of working-age people with disabilities were employed between 2010 and 2012, compared with more than 72% of the population without disabilities (U.S. Department of Labor, 2014). Looking specifically at individuals with LD, employment rates ranged from 37% (students with ASD) to 67% (students with learning disabilities; Newman et al., 2011). Although reasons for why individuals with disabilities are unemployed certainly vary from person to person, lack of sufficient education and job training are commonly cited explanations (Bureau of Labor Statistics, 2013).

> 66
> I have been in special ed all my life. Being a foster kid, I was always going to new schools and so my learning was all over the place. High school was difficult. I graduated and ended up going to a community college. That was hard. They didn't really know where I was. I ended up in this program. ... You need more time with tests, you can leave the room. I felt I was back in high school. I ended up dropping out after two semesters. I worked. I worked at some jobs that made me want to go to college. I worked at a restaurant, I worked at the mall, I worked at a movie theater. Working at a burger place, that was what made me say, no, I can't do this anymore and I really want to go to college. — *Marc Thurman* 99

Fortunately, the number of students with LD who are enrolling in higher education is increasing, as is the proportion relative to the student body as a whole (Newman, Wagner, Cameto, Knokey, & Shaver, 2010). Although the number of students in K-12 schools diagnosed with learning disabilities has actually decreased by 18% since 2002, the number of those diagnosed with ADHD and ASD is increasing dramatically (Cortiella & Horowitz, 2014). The Centers for Disease Control (CDC) recently reported that the prevalence of ASD has increased from 1 in 68 children to 1 in 59, a 150% increase since 2000 (Baio et al., 2018). And, these students plan to pursue higher education. Cameto, Levine, and Wagner (2004) noted that postsecondary education is a primary transition goal for more than 80% of high school students with disabilities. Despite increasing rates of enrollment, graduation rates have been less favorable for students with disabilities. Newman and colleagues (2011) found that 66% of college students with disabilities fail to persist to college graduation, a rate 17% higher than their peers without disabilities. Clearly, institutions of higher education who are concerned about enrollment, retention, and social justice can no longer afford to ignore this growing group of students.

In order to set the context for the book, this chapter provides an overview of the status of LD in higher education and suggests why it is imperative for college and university faculty and staff to be aware of the implications for serving this population of students. We discuss the use of specific terminology associated with LD; provide an overview of the medical, social, and legal perspectives on learning disabilities, ADHD, and ASD; and explain the implication of disability-related laws for students with LD.

Defining Disability

Because there is no consistent agreement on how disability is defined, getting an accurate count of how many people have disabilities is difficult. For example, do we count individuals identified as having an impairment (*disability*) or only those being disadvantaged because of it (*handicap*)? Such questions are controversial and make data collection challenging (Fujiura & Rutkowski-Kmitta, 2001). That said, it is estimated that more than a billion people in the world experience some form of disability. This number is likely to grow, not only because people are living longer but also because chronic physical and mental health conditions are increasing. The International Classification of Functioning, Disability, and Health (ICF), adopted as the conceptual framework for the World Health Organization (WHO), defines disability as "an umbrella term for impairments, activity limitations, and participation restrictions" (WHO, 2018, ¶1). *Disability* refers not only to the individual experience of a health condition but also to the environmental and social factors that impact the individual. It is a term used in both the educational and legal systems to signify the need for assessment, intervention, and equal treatment in educational and other settings.

From a social justice and self-advocacy perspective, negatively connoted terminology such as *disability* and *disorder*, though necessary in specific contexts, frames learning challenges only in terms of deficits and may suggest that individuals who experience them are not "normal." In contrast, the term *neurodiversity*, first coined by Judy Singer in the late 1990s, extends to all learners and suggests that neurodevelopmental differences exist on a spectrum (Pollak, 2009). Neurodiversity accounts for the individual neurological differences in human brains, but it is also associated with a social movement for ASD acceptance and can be controversial due to the differences in how the term is used.

Controversy also extends to "person-first language," or the convention of referring to "individuals with a disability or condition" rather than a "disabled person" (Dunn & Andrews, 2015). For example, this means referring to an "individual with blindness" rather than a "blind person," and it suggests one's identity is separate from the specific disability. However, within the ASD community, many reject "person with autism" for precisely this reason; essentially, many see themselves as autistic and embrace this difference as an aspect of their identity (Brown, 2011). Within the education community, ASD is the term currently used, primarily due to changes in the most recent edition of the *Diagnostic and Statistical Manual of Mental Disorders* (*DSM-5*; American Psychiatric Association, 2013), in which specific disorders such as Asperger's syndrome were subcategorized under the broad term *autism spectrum disorders*. Many use "individuals on the spectrum" as a kind of shorthand that minimizes the use of the term *autism*, which holds a negative connotation for some (Brown, 2011).

Models of Disability

Educators, policy makers, and service providers view disability from a variety of perspectives, including those of medicine, law, education, and social justice. Although each can be said to exist within a specific context and for specific purposes, these models are not mutually exclusive. Furthermore, models for understanding and assisting those with disabilities have evolved over time, due to changing societal attitudes toward disability. Significantly, as individuals with disabilities have increasingly voiced their own perspectives on the labels and terminology associated with their personhood, newer models have emerged. Our perspectives are likely to evolve further with our growing understanding of the brain and how people learn. This section includes just a few models that are currently relevant, as each contributes to the educational experiences of those with LD.

Medical Model

The medical model generally considers disability within the context of a loss or deviation from the norm, as determined by professionals qualified to make this judgment. WHO, for example, uses *impairment* to focus on limitations in functioning as compared to the general population (Fujiura & Rutkowski-Kmitta, 2001). *Disorder* suggests a condition, physical or mental, that interferes with normal functioning, and these are listed in the *Diagnostic and Statistical Manual of Mental Disorders (DSM)* for clinical coding of diagnoses. Physicians and psychiatrists use such diagnostic terminology to identify and treat patients. Though many would agree that knowing the root causes of a learning challenge is important, the medical model's emphasis on diagnosis, disorder, and disease promotes the concept that the individual is broken and needs to be fixed. This perspective has been questioned in recent years as the concept of neurological variation has come to the forefront of LD research (see Chapter 2).

In the United States, the legal and educational systems traditionally rely on the medical model. Diagnostic testing is designed to help identify specific areas of deficit that make learning and educational functioning difficult for students, and then interventions are designed to provide support for these areas. However, the majority of faculty, staff, and administrators who work with students transitioning to college do not have access to diagnostic information and have not been trained to interpret such documentation, limiting this model's usefulness in a postsecondary context.

The Rehabilitation Model

The rehabilitation model recognizes that disability is dependent on context and environment, but it also focuses on fixing what is broken. The Nagi disablement model (1965) was instrumental in introducing the term *functional limitation*, which focuses on the loss of an ability to perform one's everyday activities. For Nagi, a sociologist, a disability starts with pathology (i.e., something wrong with an individual body) that impairs the ability to perform a function in a particular context. For example, a pianist who loses a finger may not be able to perform at 100% and may lose her job, as well as the identity associated with this role. However, the pianist has a disability only in the context of playing the piano (Altman, 2001). This is also relevant to LD. In pre- or non-literate societies, dyslexia is not a disadvantage, as there is no requirement to perform the function of reading. The postsecondary accommodations model of disability support can be said to be a rehabilitation model in that students are provided with adaptive equipment and accommodations "to 'overcome' their functional limitations and accomplish their academic goals, succeed in college, and enter the workplace" (Evans, Broido, Brown, & Wilke, 2017, p. 61).

The Social Model

Arising in the 1980s, the social model of disability focused on the individual experience and represented the idea that each individual is unique and worthy, as opposed to not normal. Promoting diversity and inclusion, along with empowerment of individuals through self-advocacy, proponents of the social model reject the notion that those with disabilities are lacking or missing something (Haegele & Hodge, 2016). They argue that disability is located in an exclusionary, oppressive environment, not the body of the individual. Those working from this perspective in a college environment have been focused on access as it relates to buildings, technology, or other aspects of the curriculum. Often, they subscribe to a universal design philosophy (see Chapters 4 and 6), which can be used proactively to address barriers to access for all students, not just those with disabilities (Evans et al., 2017).

The Social Justice/Ableist Model

The social justice or ableist model of disability is aligned with the broader social justice movement that examines the concepts of privilege and oppression in order to provide insight and education on the formation of attitudes towards disability (Evans, Assadi, & Herriott, 2005). The concept of ableism, which is defined as discrimination against those with disabilities, promotes able-bodied and able-mindedness as the norm, and academia is a strong cultural reinforcer of this idea (Dolmage, 2017). With an emphasis on promoting diversity and acknowledging the intersectionality of the individual with a disability's experiences and multiple identities, the social justice approach identifies the power and privilege of the able-bodied and advocates for the end of oppression of those with disabilities (Evans et al., 2017). In a postsecondary context, the inclusion of disability as part of diversity initiatives would offer practical resources to students with disabilities, raise awareness among the college community, and contribute positively to a welcoming campus climate (see Chapter 6 for a larger discussion of diversity and inclusion efforts).

Typically, intersectionality has involved the contexts of race, ethnicity, class, and gender, but it is clear that disability and the formation of a "disability identity" are relevant to this approach (see Chapter 3 for more discussion). In addition, the factors involving disproportionality in the actual identification of LD are complex, in that some groups can be over-identified while others can be under-identified, which speaks to the overall inconsistency in this area (Morgan et al., 2015; Sparks & Lovett, 2009). Research drawing on data from the Education Longitudinal Study of 2002 (Shifrer, Muller, & Callahan, 2011) suggested that although initial results pointed to race as a key predictor of disproportionality in identification of LD, further analysis indicated that disproportionate identification is related to differences in socioeconomic status (SES), a correlate of race in the United States. How race, SES, and gender intersect with a diagnosis of LD is beyond the scope of this book, but identification is key to receiving support services, and we seem very far from achieving equity in terms of access and opportunities.

> ❝
> A lot of minority students are over-represented in special education, and they are being misdiagnosed. Some teachers see African American students act out and instead of dealing with the student one-on-one, [the student] gets labeled. They are using special education as a tool to segregate the classroom. ... Teachers don't want to deal with African American or Hispanic students. ... You can start looking at yourself differently and your self-esteem goes downhill. You're in the special ed classroom all day and the White students have their own teacher. — *Isaac Alam* ❞

College students with disabilities may have multiple identities, including experiences of both oppression and privilege, but these identities can be fluid and do not always intersect (Evans et al., 2017). Although there are different theoretical approaches to the concept of disability, the growing disability studies movement might be said to be unified based on shared experiences in the areas of "stigma, oppression, the fight for more positive representations, and the struggle for physical and intellectual access" (Dolmage, 2014, p. 20).

> **"** Because autism itself is not clearly understood by the general public, many students are loathe to self-identify, because they don't want to be viewed as a 'problem' from the start, before they even meet their faculty. There's a lot of internalized ableism that goes along with an autism diagnosis, because of negative media portrayals and attempts to make students conform to the 'norm' in their younger years. — *Sara Sanders Gardner, Autism Spectrum Navigators Program Director, Bellevue College* **"**

The Legal Model: Key Protections

The legal protections afforded individuals with disabilities in postsecondary contexts are focused on preventing discrimination and ensuring access to education. Three primary pieces of legislation are particularly relevant to the education of students with LD and those who work with them: The Individuals with Disabilities Education Act (IDEA), Section 504 of the Rehabilitation Act of 1973 (Section 504), and the Americans with Disabilities Act (ADA; see Figure 1.1). Although the importance of these laws cannot be overstated, understanding all aspects of this legislation and associated case law can be challenging for even the most seasoned professionals in disability-related fields (Lalor, 2017). Disability law has evolved over time and will continue to change. Still, it is important that faculty and administrators possess an understanding of the fundamentals of disability law and the basic philosophy of access and equity upon which the laws were developed. A brief summary of each piece of legislation is provided.

The Individuals with Disabilities Education Act. Originally enacted as the Education for All Handicapped Children Act of 1975 (Public Law 94-142), IDEA is an education law that has been amended and reauthorized over the past three decades. IDEA is known as an entitlement program, in that federal funds are provided to ensure a "free and appropriate education" in the "least restrictive environment" for all students receiving a special education until graduation from high school or the age of 22. Special education services for qualified students are outlined in an individualized education plan (IEP), a document that is signed by the special education team and the parent(s) or guardian(s) and reviewed at least once each year. However, when IDEA was amended in 2004, the focus shifted from documentation of disability to the measurement of student progress and response to intervention (RTI). This could mean that students with LD may be at a disadvantage when transitioning to college if they do not have recent documentation of their learning needs (Shaw, Keenan, Madaus, & Banerjee, 2010). Under IDEA, high school personnel develop a summary of performance (SOP) for each student, outlining not only the student's achievement and current performance abilities but also recommendations for transitioning to a postsecondary setting (IDEA, 2004).

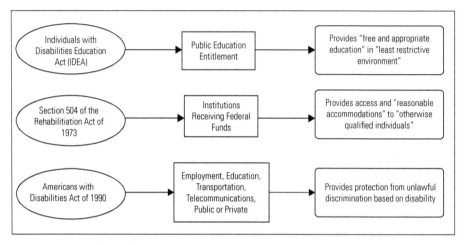

Figure 1.1. Major legislation impacting learning disabilities.

Because so many students with LD have received special education services in their K-12 education, they are familiar with the idea of receiving extra support in the form of accommodations, modifications, and services. As such, these students and their parents or guardians are sometimes under the false impression that these same accommodations, modifications, and services will carry over to higher education. To be clear, IDEA covers only K-12 education. Therefore, postsecondary institutions do not offer special education programs and are not required to provide special programs, individual support staff, modified curriculum, or even the same accommodations offered in K-12 education. The IEP may be useful in some cases to document a disability and indicate which accommodations have benefitted a student in the past, but providing a copy of the IEP to a disability support services professional does not obligate a college to provide the same services and accommodations.

For most students with LD in high school, transition planning is associated with the SOP and individualized transition plan (ITP), which are mandated by the IDEA. However, transition planning is inconsistent for many students with disabilities, and only 55% have postsecondary accommodations listed in their transition plans (Newman, Madaus, & Javitz, 2016). This is of particular note considering that having a transition plan that includes accommodations increases the likelihood of receiving accommodations in college (Newman & Madaus, 2015a).

The Americans with Disabilities Act of 1990 (ADA) is major piece of civil rights legislation that protects the rights of individuals with disabilities against discrimination in most public environments, not just schools and colleges. Of all federal legislation, the ADA provides the broadest definition of disability, particularly after revisions became effective in 2009, when it became the Americans with Disabilities Act Amendments Act (ADAAA). The ADA provides protection for an "otherwise qualified" individual who "has a physical or mental impairment that substantially limits one or more major life activity" (P.L. 110-325, 42 U.S.C. §§ 12101 et seq., 2008). Learning, reading, concentrating, and thinking are now identified as major life activities, meaning LDs are covered by this law (Shaw & Dukes, 2013).

Section 504 of the Rehabilitation Act. Section 504 is another civil rights law that provides access to any program that is federally funded if the individual is "otherwise qualified." As such, both K-12 and postsecondary institutions must offer "reasonable accommodations" in order to provide educational access (29 U.S.C. §794). Section 504 applies to all public and private institutions that accept federal funds. For example, institutions that offer federal financial aid or accept federal grants must abide by Section 504. For students with LD, the ADA and Section 504 can be considered interchangeable in their protection against discrimination, but many parents of students with disabilities in secondary school are more familiar with Section 504 because they have heard of "504 plans" and mistakenly believe these will transfer to the college setting (Shaw & Dukes, 2013). To be clear, they do not transfer to college. In college, a disability services provider will use an interactive process or dialogue with the student to determine eligibility for specific academic adjustments, auxiliary aids, or other accommodations. As part of that process, students may provide copies of any plans from secondary school (e.g., 504 plan, IEP) for consideration in the determination of accommodations.

An important provision under the ADA and Section 504 that students and their families need to understand is the idea of a "reasonable" accommodation, which relates not only to what a postsecondary institution can financially afford to provide but also to what the student needs based on individual diagnosis and profile. Although some students may be used to receiving accommodations in high school, such as extra time on tests or extensions on assignments, disability staff may determine, based on available documentation, that these accommodations are not appropriate given the documented condition.

Additionally, the student with LD must be "otherwise qualified" and meet the same standards of specific programs as other students if they are deemed essential to the program of study. For example, a specific level of math is required for many health profession tracks because the ability to understand and titrate medication dosages is considered essential to the program and professional field. Determinations of what is an essential element of a program are made on an institution-by-institution or program-by-program basis.

Colleges and universities are all required to follow these legal stipulations, but disability services can vary from a single disability support staff member charged with reviewing documentation and determining accommodations to robust programs offering tutoring, learning strategy instruction, and assistive technology instruction in addition to accommodations (Madaus, 2005). Generally, the Office of Civil Rights, the agency that enforces the ADA and Section 504, defers to the judgment of an institution when it shows due diligence in discussing and evaluating the appropriateness of an accommodation within the context of academic and program requirements. Although colleges and universities are legally mandated to offer accommodations to students with disabilities, students need to initiate the process and identify themselves to the institution through the disability support services (DSS) office or accessibility office (see Chapter 3).

Conclusion

It is the purpose of this book to provide guidance for college and university faculty and staff who will encounter these students, who are often at risk, in their professional capacities. We believe that having a framework for understanding the neurodevelopmental patterns that impact learning can assist educators in identifying strategies for individual learners and in establishing an accessible and inclusive environment (see Chapters 2 and 4). Faculty should also be aware of the legal basis for accommodations in the postsecondary setting and how the accommodations process should work (see Chapter 3). We also discuss the experiences of students with LD outside the classroom and how professionals can better serve these students in the cocurriculum (see Chapter 5). Finally, we believe that the transition to college can be smoother for students with LD if a range of institutional or programmatic approaches are considered, and we outline some of these in Chapter 6.

Chapter 2
Who Are the Students With LD?

Despite variability in terminology, it is critical that postsecondary educators and administrators be able to identify and understand students with LD. They need to know how the characteristics of these students impact planning and delivering educational services, in and outside the classroom. How should institutions of higher learning support these students? What special considerations and programming promote successful transition and retention for students who learn differently? In this chapter, we begin by surveying how recent advances in neuroscience have shaped our understanding of LD, evolving from a medical model focused on cognitive deficits to a diversity model that acknowledges strengths as well as challenges. This elevates the status of students with LD from a marginalized group who require special considerations to rightful contributing members of the academic community. Next, we review specific profiles of students with LD, keeping in mind that many students will not be officially identified as such in postsecondary settings. We also discuss their characteristic challenges and strengths and the ways educators can improve students' learning outcomes even when they are not officially recognized by the institution as eligible for accommodations.

The New Neuroscience of Disability

Why should educators bother to learn about the neuroscience that describes the cognitive profiles we call LD? Perhaps the most significant reason is to discredit the commonly held notion that the construct of LD (including ADHD and ASD) was invented to confer unfair advantages on certain groups or individuals. We have a growing body of neuroscience to validate the existence of LD in terms of scientifically measurable differences in brain development, anatomy, and behavior. Furthermore, recent research on the complexities of LD highlights characteristic strengths as well as deficits, supporting a paradigm shift that allows viewing these profiles through the lens of cognitive neurodiversity rather than disability/deficit alone. In terms of planning, practice, and program evaluation, educators will benefit from knowing the research on factors (both confounding and protective) that influence outcomes so they can develop interventions that promote optimal learning.

The field of cognitive neuroscience has burgeoned in the past 20 years, propelled by new technologies and lines of research that illuminate our understanding of how learning occurs. Advances in genetics, brain imaging, and behavioral science have altered our understanding of brain specialization and variation and of the factors that facilitate or hinder efficient learning. This section provides a brief layperson's overview of the neurobiology of disability, outlining recent research trends and findings.

Genetics

Advances in the study of genetics support the common notion that "the apple doesn't fall far from the tree" when it comes to LD. Studies that confirm the strong heritability of reading difficulty, the most researched of the LDs (Fiedorowicz et al., 2001), suggest that dyslexia represents a persistent, well-characterized pattern of brain organization that can be traced through familial connections. In lay terms, approximately half the children of a parent with reading disability will themselves have reading disability (Fiedorowicz et al., 2001). Although we may not understand all the factors that contribute to reading difficulty, the accumulating evidence from twin studies and genome analysis helps establish the verifiable reality of this genotype. Similarly, studies show the high heritability of ADHD (ADHD Institute, 2017) and of ASD (Sandin et al., 2017), establishing a basis for possible early identification and intervention.

Although research suggests that certain combinations of genes predispose individuals to the hallmark characteristics of LD, scientists believe there are no genes that solely result in these specific conditions (Fiedorowicz et al., 2001). Rather, these genes are likely to affect more global behaviors related to language, processing speed, attention, and executive function, which are factors in learning for all individuals, regardless of disability status. Moreover, the expression of genes may vary in response to environmental conditions (Fiedorowicz et al., 2001). This helps explain the wide individual variability of characteristics within the diagnostic categories. It is important for educators to realize that students with LD can show a range of behaviors that may not fit neatly into predetermined diagnostic categories. Research into the causes of what we traditionally call learning disabilities can shed light on how to enhance learning for all students, not just those designated LD.

Neurophysiology and Brain Imaging

Complementing genetic research, studies of neuroanatomy and neurofunction provide strong evidence that the brains of individuals with LD look and perform differently than those of neurotypicals in a variety of areas (Fiedorowicz et al., 2001). The pace of research has accelerated with the development of sophisticated neuroimaging techniques over the past 20 years. As a result, we now have a window into how brains actually function that was unimaginable a few decades ago. Research based on these technologies demonstrates atypical neural anatomy and activity in brain areas already associated with characteristics of LD.

Brain Plasticity and Protective Factors

Although there are clear genetic bases for the brain profiles we call learning disability, ADHD, and ASD, recent research on brain plasticity and resilience counters the notion that biology is destiny. It is now clear that brains remain plastic, or malleable, throughout the lifespan, constantly reorganizing neural pathways in response to experience and education. Although the most rapid growth and change occurs in the early years, the process continues as humans age. The brain is constantly reshaped by learning. Ongoing brain development provides a strong rationale for the efficacy of remedial and supportive interventions designed for college students and older adults (Kolb, Gibb, & Robinson, 2003).

Exciting research on resilience, or resistance to the adverse effects of an inherited predisposition, has uncovered a number of protective factors that predict favorable learning outcomes. Neurocognitive resilience is defined as the ability to adapt to adversity or stress in the environment by bending but not breaking (Haft & Hoeft, 2016). Positive internal characteristics that promote resilience include high levels of motivation and executive functions, strong oral language or motor skills, vocabulary, and verbal reasoning. Positive external factors include family cohesion and support as well as positive peer and school experiences. This research suggests ways to design programs that promote success for individuals with learning disabilities, ADHD, or ASD based not only on specific cognitive interventions but also on creating systems for social–emotional support while strengthening an individual's self-awareness and self-regulation through activities that foster metacognition (awareness of one's thinking processes).

Reframing Disability as Diversity

The disability rights movement has shifted the conversation from one of compensation to one of empowerment, renaming *disabled* as *differently abled*. This is desirable from a social justice perspective, but it also seems fair to ask whether this approach is justified by neurobiological evidence, so that the cognitive profiles we call "learning (dis)abilities" can be reframed as difference or diversity as opposed to deficit or pathology. In the early 1980s, less than 20 years after the term *learning disability* was first coined, leaders from the fields of education, neurology, and cognitive psychology began to address this question. This is important because terminology matters: It shapes our perspectives and attitudes regarding students with LD in college settings. Evidence drawn from these scientific fields lends credibility to those who advocate a diversity model that highlights the value of welcoming students who learn differently to the academy.

Early Neurobiological Speculations

In 1981, Margaret Rawson, an educator who pioneered research and advocacy in the field of dyslexia, addressed the question, introducing the term *diversity* to the discussion of learning disabilities. In her groundbreaking paper, "A Diversity Model for Dyslexia," she argued that the unique combination of strengths and challenges that make up any individual, due to inherited traits and responses to environmental stimuli, represents normal biological variation as well as a "diversity which is of adaptive and creative value to the person, the culture, and the race" (Rawson, 1981, p. 23). Furthermore, if we consider dyslexia as diversity, this changes the way we view and speak about dyslexics in a way that is "both liberating and productive" (p. 32).

At the same time, other neuroscientists speculated that the paradoxically high frequency of certain conditions like dyslexia, which superficially seem to convey only evolutionary disadvantages, is explained by the concurrent presence of other advantages. For example, sickle cell anemia is accompanied by resistance to malaria as well as a predisposition to a specific illness (Geschwind, 1984). In the case of dyslexia, Geschwind cites the frequent co-occurrence of advantageous visual–spatial and artistic skills and suggests that the very differences in the brain that cause difficulty when reading and writing appear to be correlated with other changes that promote visual–spatial superiority. Advantages conferred by the dyslexic brain help explain the high prevalence rates and worldwide persistence of dyslexia across languages and cultures. This concept is highly important for educators. First, it underscores the value that students with LD can add to programs and classes by virtue of their skills and talents. Second, it suggests ways to design academic and social environments that capitalize on students' specific strengths while minimizing their weaknesses. Finally, it provides a strong rationale for reframing the academic discourse on LD from the medical–deficit model to the diversity–advantages model.

The Dyslexic Advantage and Other Strengths-Based Perspectives

The scientific support for a diversity model of LD received a boost with the publication of *The Dyslexic Advantage: Unlocking the Hidden Potential of the Dyslexic Brain* (Eide & Eide, 2012), which presents the claim that the dyslexic brain represents a specific pattern of neural organization that predisposes individuals to certain abilities as well as challenges. The authors cited research that identifies four areas in which dyslexics tend to be superior to typical learners: (a) visual, spatial, and hands-on skills focused on three-dimensional objects; (b) interconnected reasoning, or seeing connections that others do not; (c) ability to bring memory fragments to bear on solution finding; and (d) dynamic ability to predict patterns accurately. However, Sally Shaywitz, a noted dyslexia researcher who founded the Yale Center for Dyslexia and Creativity, warned against proclaiming that "all dyslexics have a special talent … for most children with dyslexia, particularly during their school years, their slow reading and poor spelling present significant disadvantages" (Shaywitz, 2013, ¶3). The consensus in the field is that an accurate picture of dyslexia will clearly identify both the struggles and the potential advantages.

Meanwhile, disability-as-diversity movements have taken hold in the study of ADHD and ASD as well as dyslexia. Intriguing research identified a large group of individuals with ADHD among highly successful CEOs and entrepreneurs who are fueled by their high levels of energy and creativity and their abilities to think outside the box, thrive in high-stress situations, and take risks in pursuit of success. A notable article in *Forbes* magazine raised the question, "What do business mogul Sir Richard Branson, Ikea founder Ingvar Kamprad, and JetBlue founder David Neeleman, have in common?" The answer is that they all have ADHD. "It's why so many high-profile achievers are beginning to publicly embrace their diagnoses of ADHD" (Archer, 2014, ¶1).

The ASD self-advocacy movement also promotes the notion that individuals on the spectrum contribute unique insights and skills to society. At a presentation delivered at Landmark College in April 2018, John Elder Robison, noted author and ASD advocate, proclaimed, "We are not broken versions of some asshole's version of normal. We are a whole and necessary part of the human species" (Robison, 2018). Individuals with ASD bring characteristic strengths in many areas, including the skills and predispositions that contribute to scholarly success in academia, such as attention to details, excellent memory for facts and figures, and passionate interest and specialist knowledge on chosen topics. Temple Grandin, noted animal biologist and ASD advocate, answered the rhetorical question, What would have happened to the human species without ASD individuals, with "you'd have a bunch of people standing around in a cave, chatting and socializing and not getting anything done" (Grandin, 2014).

Profiles of Students Who Learn Differently

Students with learning disabilities, ADHD, and ASD share many characteristics, so it often makes sense to consider their aggregate presence in higher education. However, each of these diagnostic profiles also includes distinctive strengths and challenges. Understanding these differences is particularly important when planning and delivering academic programs and services that optimize the chance of academic success for students with LD. When it comes to effectively serving students with LD, one size most definitely does NOT fit all.

Dyslexia and Language-Based Learning Disabilities

Language, both oral and written, is the coin of the realm of academia, the medium through which the message is delivered from teacher to student and back again. Difficulties related to understanding and expressing linguistic information impose consistent barriers to academic success. Therefore, students with a language-based learning disability, including dyslexia (specific disability in reading) and dysgraphia (specific disability in writing), face significant challenges in the classroom and beyond. This section looks at the characteristic academic strengths and difficulties of students who are dyslexic or have a related disorder in reading or writing.

Students with reading difficulties have traditionally comprised 75%-80% of students who receive K-12 special education services under the category of learning disability (Learning Disabilities Association of America, n.d.c). The International Dyslexia Association (n.d.b) suggested that 15%-20% of the population as a whole have some of the symptoms of dyslexia, including slow or inaccurate reading, poor spelling, poor writing, or mixing up similar words. Many of these individuals are not impacted severely enough to qualify for special education. Nevertheless, they are likely to struggle with many aspects of academic learning while never receiving specialized services or accommodations. Recognizing signs of these struggles among our non-identified college students will help educators design instruction and programs for the wide range of learners in today's classrooms. Furthermore, identifying these struggles can help postsecondary personnel direct students to appropriate campus services (e.g., writing center, tutoring, disability services). A section detailing how to refer students for evaluation and appropriate services follows the discussion of specific cognitive profiles.

Neurobiological basis of dyslexia. Human brains evolved long before the invention of literacy. Therefore, there are no hardwired centers in the brain specifically designed for reading, as there are for understanding and producing oral language. Instead, the areas of the brain involved in reading have been recruited from other, evolutionarily older areas designed for processing oral language and visual information. Researchers have identified a number of specific neurobiological correlates of dyslexia that suggest a persistent pattern of brain organization and cognitive profile associated with this condition. The International Dyslexia Association Fact Sheet (International Dyslexia Association, n.d.a) identifies these as

- several genetic variants associated with dyslexic symptoms,
- absence of expected left/right-hemisphere asymmetry in specific language processing areas (planum temporale),
- ectopias or cell structure abnormalities that result from atypical migration of neurons in the developing brain,
- lower volumes of white and gray matter in specific left-hemisphere language areas,
- different patterns of left/right-hemisphere activation while reading and performing other language tasks, and
- differences in specific metabolites (i.e., brain chemicals that facilitate communication among neurons).

What are signs that a college student may be dyslexic? Difficulty learning to read and spell is the hallmark of young students with dyslexia, whose challenges often become apparent in the primary grades. College students with dyslexia may:

- need extra time to read or write,

- have trouble following directions,
- have difficulty taking notes from lectures and discussions,
- produce first drafts that are sparse and filled with mechanical and spelling errors,
- offer written responses that do not reflect the caliber of thinking shown in class, and
- have significant trouble with foreign languages.

In some ways, students with dyslexia are less visible than they were 20 years ago. College classes do not often require oral reading, which may be slow and dysfluent. Slower readers may be able to complete reading assignments using built-in accessibility software that reads texts aloud on their laptops or phones. Assignments prepared and submitted digitally, with the aid of spelling and grammar correction tools, are now the norm, making it easier for students with dyslexia to blend in. By the time students reach college, they may be experts in passing as neurotypical, claiming to have "left my reading glasses home" if called on to read aloud.

Furthermore, many students have cultivated their strengths in discussion and debate or visual processing to compensate for difficulties in processing print-based information. If faculty members give pop quizzes that require writing a few sentences or paragraphs by hand in a relatively short time, they may suspect a language-based deficit if they see students who participate knowledgeably in discussions and activities flounder, fail to complete the quiz, or hand in what looks like an illegible scrawl filled with incomplete thoughts or misspelled words.

Students whose dyslexia was diagnosed and remediated early often become competent readers and adequate spellers, but dyslexia is not cured; subtle impacts linger in reading speed and stamina and fluency of written expression. Anecdotally, students in college report that it requires more time and effort to complete typical reading and writing assignments. Empirically, researchers have used eye-tracking studies to show that even well-remediated adults with dyslexia process print more slowly and inefficiently, making reading more labor intensive and tiring (Desroches, Joanisse, & Robertson, 2006).

In addition to the challenges of academic reading, students with dyslexia typically find academic writing difficult, especially under timed conditions such as in-class essays and exams. Academic writing requires the ability to maintain focus on intellectual processes, such as generating and sequencing ideas or considering audience and purpose, while executing more mechanical processes such as accurate spelling and punctuation. This proves to be a major challenge for students with language-processing deficits (Berninger, Nielsen, & Raskind, 2008). Taking adequate and usable class notes, which requires simultaneous receptive (i.e., listening) and expressive (i.e., writing) language processing, is often extremely difficult, as is studying a foreign language (Ganschow, Sparks, & Javorsky, 1998). Students with dyslexia who are sometimes granted foreign language waivers in high school find themselves severely disadvantaged in college or graduate school, where waivers are increasingly difficult to obtain and foreign language study is considered a fundamental component of the curriculum.

66 I have dyslexia and oral language difficulties and have particular difficulty with written and oral expression. So it may not be surprising that papers requiring collecting ideas, critiquing ideas, and combining ideas into new thinking are very hard. As someone with difficulties in writing process and oral language expression, I can work for hours and accumulate a lot of information but have a lot of trouble with taking the information and drawing original ideas about it. Because of language expression issues, I also have trouble rewording ideas so that the ideas sound like my own. I often feel like the only option is to essentially copy somebody else's ideas. I feel overwhelmed and exasperated because written expression requires attention, fine motor skills, processing and interpreting language and visual stimulation, and organizing thoughts into written text. — *Andrea* 99

Dyscalculia

Dyscalculia (Greek *dys* = poor; *calculia* = counting), difficulty in learning or performing arithmetic, is a relatively recently recognized specific learning disability. The term *dyscalculia* itself is controversial and is used informally to refer to common math difficulties with simple calculations or in learning basic math facts like the times tables. However, researchers in the field use it to refer to a specific, brain-based deficit in numeracy, or number sense, a foundational cognitive process that makes it possible to estimate and compare quantities quickly. This underlying deficit is thought to influence the ability to represent quantities symbolically as abstract concepts (e.g., numbers or letters). Although it does not have the global impact on academic and behavioral areas seen with dyslexia, ADHD, or ASD, dyscalculia creates significant challenges in math and science courses that may be required for graduation and are often gateways for a variety of career choices in medicine, technology, and economics.

Number sense is located in specific areas of the brain. The intraparietal sulcus, an area associated with mathematical processing, appears to show less gray matter and less activation in individuals diagnosed with dyscalculia than in neurotypicals. Other parietal and frontal areas may also be involved (Wilson, n.d.). Still controversial, because of the lack of longitudinal studies, is whether these differences represent a developmental lag or an ingrained deficit.

Research by Butterworth and others suggests a prevalence of 5%-8% in the general population and across a wide range of IQs. Dyscalculia often co-occurs with dyslexia and ADHD (Soares & Patel, 2015). Contrary to popular thinking that "girls are not good at math," it seems to affect males and females equally (D'Arcangelo, 2001).

Like dyslexia, dyscalculia may be recognized first by teachers in early grades, as students struggle to keep up with peers in foundational skills. College personnel are unlikely to be the ones who diagnose dyscalculia, but they are in a position to refer students for evaluation and services if they see persistent signs of dyscalculia consistent with the patterns of math performance described in Figure 2.1. See the end of this chapter for appropriate ways to discuss this possibility with students.

Dyscalculia Checklist
- Shows difficulty understanding concepts of place value, quantity, number lines, positive and negative value, carrying and borrowing
- Has difficulty understanding and doing word problems
- Has difficulty sequencing information or events
- Exhibits difficulty using steps involved in math operations
- Shows difficulty understanding fractions
- Is challenged making change and handling money
- Displays difficulty recognizing patterns when adding, subtracting, multiplying, or dividing
- Has difficulty putting language to math processes
- Has difficulty understanding concepts related to time such as days, weeks, months, seasons, quarters, etc.
- Exhibits difficulty organizing problems on the page, keeping numbers lined up, following through on long division problems

---

Figure 2.1. Dyscalculia checklist. Adapted from "Dyscalculia Checklist" (Dyscalculia.org., n.d.b)

Dyscalculia challenges and strengths. Students who are dyscalculic may excel in many other academic areas and, paradoxically, sometimes at conceptual math or in certain branches of math like geometry or statistics. Math and science courses present the greatest challenges to these students, but telltale characteristics of dyscalculia may also interfere with day-to-day functioning. Students may show unusual difficulties in telling time using analog clocks, estimating how much time it will take to complete assignments, or determining when to leave in order to make scheduled appointments. Financial situations such as keeping track of credit card and debit card transactions and other personal finances as well as shopping with cash and coins can be problematic. Following directions that involve numbers such as a street address or ZIP code or that involve directionality (e.g., left vs. right) may cause difficulty. Individuals with dyscalculia also may have difficulty remembering schedules or sequences of events (for timelines or summarizing narratives), reading musical notation, learning choreographed dance steps, or measuring ingredients for recipes or materials for construction (Frye, n.d.).

66 The learning difference I have makes math rocket science for me. If you were to place a geometry or algebra problem in front of me and give me no help, chances are it would take me hours to solve it. The problems are a bunch of shapes and numbers to me and do not make any sense whatsoever. Therefore, I try to make sense of it but often end up with the wrong answer and a pounding migraine. — *Megan Fabianski* 99

Attention-Deficit/Hyperactivity Disorder (ADHD)

The diagnosis of attention-deficit/hyperactivity disorder (ADHD) has been subject to skepticism and controversy in the popular press. Is it real? Is it overdiagnosed? Does it falsely categorize normal behaviors as pathological? This section addresses these concerns while exploring this profile as an example of cognitive diversity.

ADHD was originally thought to be a childhood behavioral disorder, typically outgrown by the teen years. By the early 1990s, changes in understanding and diagnosing this condition had profound implications for students, parents, and educators, as it became apparent that ADHD persisted into adolescence and adulthood (Richard, 1995). Whereas specific learning disabilities such as dyslexia and dyscalculia manifest themselves predominantly in academic settings, ADHD affects behaviors across many domains: academic, familial, social, and vocational. Nevertheless, recognition of the profile we now call ADHD first emerged in school settings as the current model for education became dominant, including highly routinized school days that commit students to physically passive but mentally challenging activities for long blocks of time.

It has been noted that symptoms tend to evolve over time, with young children showing more hyperactive behaviors and older children and adults displaying more internal restlessness and inattention. According to prominent researchers such as Thomas H. Brown and Russell Barkley, this characterization ignores the fundamental nature of ADHD, which should be understood as a disorder of self-regulation and might be better named executive function disorder (Barkley, 1998; Brown, 2005).

Executive function and self-regulation. Barkley and Brown both saw attention and impulsivity as symptoms of developmental differences in the neural networks that manage inhibition and self-control, including the ability to defer immediate gratification in the service of long-term goals (Barkley, 1998; Brown, 2005). To clarify commonly used terminology, *self-regulation* is one's ability to persist in goal-directed behavior over time, even in the face of distractions and frustrations, and *executive function* (EF) is the collection of brain-based cognitive processes that support that ability. These processes are involved in planning, remembering, inhibiting or delaying responding, and shifting attention or focusing on something now to achieve something later (Barkley, 1997). In functional terms, these deficits result in difficulties developing realistic plans, remembering goals, activating and sustaining effort over time, and regulating emotional responses to life's daily frustrations (Parker & Boutelle, 2009).

What this means for students with ADHD is that their transition to postsecondary settings is complicated, over and above the challenges other first-year students face, by the specific nature of their cognitive profiles. At a time when the predictable daily structure provided by parents and secondary school is no longer available, students have to navigate an increasingly complex academic, physical, and social environment; an academic schedule that is highly variable from day to day; assignments that are increasingly long-term rather than daily; a bewildering choice of cocurricular activities; classes and activities where they encounter more diverse students and faculty than in high school; and, in many cases, a campus that is geographically challenging, spread across many different buildings and offices. Whereas most entering students grapple with balancing newfound freedoms against newly conferred responsibilities, students with ADHD arrive on campus equipped with neural mechanisms that provide less internal scaffolding for making good transitions without external support.

Neurobiological basis for ADHD. A brief overview of neural mechanisms illuminates the added challenges that students with ADHD experience during transitions. As with dyslexia, advances in genetics and neuroimaging provide evidence of several neurobiological features of ADHD that account for the distinctive cognitive profile. Neurologists have long associated the prefrontal cortex, parts of the cerebellum, and parts of the basal ganglia with executive functions, and these regions tend to be smaller in individuals with ADHD (Swanson, Castellanos, Murias, LaHoste, & Kennedy, 1998). These size differences are most likely caused by several genetic variants and mutations, as ADHD proves to be highly heritable, with a heritability of up to .80, meaning that 80% of the differences between individuals with ADHD and those without ADHD are attributable to genetic factors (ADHD Institute, 2017). Like dyslexia, a number of different genes are implicated in ADHD, rather than a single gene. Genes that regulate dopamine, a neurotransmitter that carries information across neurons, appear to be involved, as imaging studies indicate reduced levels of dopamine activity in regions of the brain that regulate attention and self-regulation. Importantly, research has also ruled out dietary factors, faulty parenting, and excessive TV watching as causes of ADHD (Barkley, 1998).

The executive functions are among the last to mature, developing well into an individual's mid-20s. As a result, long-term goal-directed tasks can be challenging for most adolescents and young adults. One important benefit of learning about the role of EF in students with ADHD is that educators can apply that knowledge to improve academic and programmatic success for the wide range of entering students likely to experience some difficulty in those areas. Over and above the usual age-related issues, students diagnosed with ADHD appear to lag behind their chronological-aged peers, perhaps as much as 30%, in the rate at which EF circuits in the brain mature (Berger, Slobodin, Aboud, Melamed, & Cassuto, 2013).

In practical terms, this means that an 18-year-old first-year college student with ADHD might have the EF capabilities of a typically maturing 12-year-old.

Medication issues. Differences in neurotransmitter levels are the basis for the medical interventions available for ADHD in the form of psychostimulants or antidepressants such as Ritalin and Adderall. These medications help increase the usable amount of the chemicals that are essential for the flow of information across different brain regions. In turn, this boosts the capacity to inhibit and regulate impulsive or distractible behaviors, such that 70%-90% of children show improved behavior when taking ADHD medications (Barkley, 1998). However, difficulties around effective use of medication are one of the issues students with ADHD may bring to campus. One key question for incoming students is whether to seek a new prescribing physician near the college or university or to depend on visits to home physicians over breaks to monitor medication use. Students probably relied on parents to keep their supplies of medication current or to monitor side effects or changes in effectiveness that occur over time or in response to new task demands. Keeping supplies of medication secure may also be an issue. Students have been known to be casual about sharing their medications with peers, sometimes selling them on a campus black market for stimulants, especially around exam time.

Assessment of ADHD. Although ADHD is commonly diagnosed in childhood, growing recognition of its persistence into adulthood has resulted in the identification of more college-aged students with ADHD (Brown, 2005). Thomas Brown is an important spokesperson for this group of students, who may have performed adequately in high school but who begin to unravel when faced with the increased academic and social task demands of higher education. He has championed greater understanding of adult ADHD among college and university personnel, offering educators practical guidance for increasing persistence and retention of these students while helping students and their parents or guardians develop better self-awareness and survival strategies.

Unlike dyslexia, which is usually diagnosed by educational psychologists, ADHD is most often diagnosed by medical professionals (i.e., pediatricians and psychiatrists). Instead of a battery of psychoeducational tests of language, memory, and academic achievement, ADHD is generally diagnosed using structured interviews, following a protocol in the *DSM-5* (American Psychiatric Association, 2013). A thorough assessment includes interviews of parents and teachers and, in some cases, observations of the client, especially in school settings.

The *DSM-5* lists many examples of ADHD characteristics (see Figure 2.2). The frequently included term *often* underscores the fact that ADHD behavior may be inconsistent: An individual's performance may vary dramatically from day to day. Most people experience some of these "symptoms" some of the time, but the *DSM-5* stipulates that in order to qualify for a diagnosis, individuals must exhibit significantly more severe and more frequent manifestations of these behaviors than chronological peers, and these behaviors must cause disruptive difficulties at school, work, or in social settings (American Psychiatric Association, 2013).

Selected Characteristics of ADHD
- Fails to pay close attention to details or makes careless mistakes in schoolwork, at work, or during other activities (e.g., overlooks or misses details, work is inaccurate)
- Has difficulty sustaining attention in tasks or play activities (e.g., has difficulty remaining focused during lectures, conversations, or lengthy reading)
- Has difficulty following through on instructions
- Is reluctant to engage in tasks that require sustained mental effort or attention

Examples of Hyperactive-Impulsive Behavior
- Often fidgets with or taps hands or feet or squirms in seat
- Is often "on the go," acting as if "driven by a motor" (e.g., is unable to be or is uncomfortable being still for extended time, as in restaurants, meetings; may be experienced by others as being restless or difficult to keep up with)
- Often has difficulty waiting his or her turn (e.g., while waiting in line)
- Often interrupts or intrudes on others (e.g., butts into conversations, games, or activities; may start using other people's things without asking or receiving permission; for adolescents and adults, may intrude into or take over what others are doing)

Figure 2.2. Selected characteristics of ADHD identified in the *DSM-5* (American Psychiatric Association, 2013).

What are the signs that a college student may have ADHD? The most obvious signs of ADHD in postsecondary students, whether diagnosed or not, are also the difficulties reported by Kent and colleagues (2011) among high school students with ADHD: failure to complete or turn in assignments on time, increased tardiness and absences, lower GPAs, and higher rate of course failure (in DuPaul, Dahlstrom-Hakki, et al., 2017; see also Figure 2.3). School personnel often assume these behaviors reflect lack of motivation or commitment; however, reframing them as cognitive issues and, therefore, responsive to interventions is critical to designing supportive programs.

Common Signs of ADHD in College Students
- Failure to complete assignments, despite obvious command of necessary skills
- Great difficulty keeping appointments, meeting deadlines, balancing personal with academic demands
- Disorganized materials or thoughts
- Distractible/fidgety or excessive daydreaming in class
- Emotionally over-reactive: irritable, frustrated, agitated
- Impulsive comments and actions
- Difficulty focusing on reading unless highly interesting
- Difficulty organizing and revising written assignments, especially longer papers
- Difficulty staying on topic during discussions

Figure 2.3. Common signs of ADHD in college students.

High levels of EF are critical to many specifically academic tasks, such as reading, writing, tracking discussions, and taking notes. Students with ADHD often have particular problems with reading stamina, losing focus or falling asleep after just a few pages unless the text is highly compelling (Hecker, Burns, Katz, Elkind, & Elkind, 2002). Organizing writing assignments is often especially challenging even when students have strong expressive language skills. Students may be flooded with ideas but experience great difficulty prioritizing and sequencing them and may struggle to schedule the many subtasks involved in producing substantial academic papers. Students with ADHD typically miss assignment deadlines or wait until the last moment to get started, resulting in papers that do not reflect their command of the content. Taking class notes can be overwhelming as students struggle to inhibit distractions or fail to sustain the effort and focus required to capture in writing the gist of a lecture or discussion (DuPaul, Dahlstrom-Hakki, et al., 2017).

" Time management is crucial — it is so easy to get behind because of the lack of structured time at college; setting up and following a schedule can be really helpful. Students also need to know how they learn best. For instance, some students I know listen to their lectures over again in order to comprehend and retain the information, while others learn more from reading. — *Elizabeth Hamblet, Learning Specialist, Columbia University Disability Services Office* "

" My attention span was a big struggle for me. I felt that I was 10 steps behind everyone else in class. School had always been a struggle for me. I could not pay attention at all, but I had no idea it was because of my learning disability. While everyone in my class was paying attention, I was playing with pencils under my desk. I was placed in a special education class at a young age, which only contributed to my low self-esteem when it came to learning. Being segregated by the so-called "normal" children and being made fun of by my siblings was the icing on the cake from my fear of education. I was eventually placed in a regular education class, but I still struggled. — *Ryan November* "

Emotional regulation is a key executive function. Therefore, difficulty calibrating emotional responses to a situation may also be a sign of ADHD. Students with ADHD may appear over-reactive, exhibiting irritability, frustration, or agitation in situations others take in stride. Their frontal lobes are hijacked by their emotions, precluding a moderate response.

They often have trouble putting a difficult situation on the "back burner" so they can attend to other task demands such as participating appropriately in class (Parker & Boutelle, 2009).

College students with ADHD are also more prone to substance abuse and other high-risk behaviors and are more likely to smoke tobacco (Wilens, 2004). Students who are undiagnosed or recently diagnosed with ADHD run a greater risk for substance abuse than those who were diagnosed earlier and treated with appropriate stimulant medication (Biederman et al., 2008). It is worth noting that ADHD is highly comorbid with a number of affective disorders such as anxiety, depression, and eating disorders, making it difficult to tease out and treat the root causes of these problematic behaviors (Biederman et al., 2007).

In addition to academic difficulties, college students with ADHD may experience trouble with peer relationships, sustaining friendships, participating consistently in sports and other cocurricular activities, and regulating their sleep and spending habits. They have difficulty holding down student jobs and are more likely to experience legal difficulties than peers without ADHD (Brown, 2005).

Autism Spectrum Disorder (ASD)

Students with ASD have much to offer the academic community if they can navigate the many challenges precipitated by their atypical perceptions and behaviors. As things stand now, they enroll in postsecondary institutions at rates close to their neurotypical peers but earn fewer credits and degrees. According to a U.S. Department of Education longitudinal study, 47% of young adults with ASD enrolled in a postsecondary institution within six years of graduating from high school, but only 35% earned a degree, a notably lower completion rate than the 51% for the general population (Shmulsky & Gobbo, 2013).

Neurobiological basis of ASD. As with other neurodevelopmental profiles considered to impact learning (e.g., dyslexia and ADHD), research has established a genetic basis for many incidences of ASD. More than 1,000 genes may be implicated as risk factors (National Institutes of Health, 2017), along with a larger-than-typical incidence of spontaneous mutations that are not inherited (Meade-Kelly, 2013). Overall, however, the heritability of ASD has been estimated at about 60%, with up to 40% of heritability related to environmental factors such as exposure to chemicals and age of parents at conception (Centers for Disease Control and Prevention, 2016). The brain development of people with ASD varies from individual to individual, but some people with ASD have more neurons than typical and show overgrowth in parts of the outer surface of the brain (i.e., the cortex) as well as patchy areas where the normal structure of the cortex layers is disturbed. These variations occur in the frontal and temporal lobes of the cortex, predominantly in right-hemisphere areas involved in processing emotions, social behavior, and some aspects of language. They are thought to underlie the differences in socialization, communication, and cognitive functioning characteristic of people with ASD (CDC, 2016).

Assessment of ASD. Diagnosing ASD can be difficult because there is no medical test, like a blood test, to identify it. Clinicians look at the individual's overall behavior and development to make a diagnosis. Typically, this is done by a pediatrician, since ASD can be detected when young children fail to reach developmental milestones for language, social, and motor skills. For a two-year-old, a diagnosis by an experienced professional can be considered very reliable. However, many children do not receive a final diagnosis until they are much older. This delay means that children with ASD might not get the early help they need, especially to navigate increasingly complex social interactions with peers (CDC, 2016).

Challenges and strengths in college settings. Although individuals with ASD vary in language and social ability from severely affected to high functioning, students who make it to college are most likely to be toward the higher end of intellectual and language competence. The type of autism they exhibit is sometimes called the "Little Professor Syndrome" because individuals may be highly expert on a narrow topic of interest, a trait that is usually valued in academia. However, the term is not complimentary because it suggests the often-caricatured absentminded and eccentric kind of professor—pedantic and lacking social skills. Prince-Hughes (2003), an anthropology professor who identifies as having Asperger's, lamented that although professors' expertise may be seen in a positive light, students with the same traits "are often pushed from the one place (academia) that can maximize our potential and give our lives meaning" (p. B16).

Why do these academically talented students fail to thrive at college? At core, according to the *DSM-5*, ASD is a neurobiologically based difficulty with social communication, often characterized by strong, narrowly focused interests or repetitive behaviors and sometimes accompanied by unusual sensitivity to sounds, lights, smells, and tactile sensations (APA, 2013). Because of disturbances in right-hemisphere brain organization, individuals with ASD tend to have difficulty processing rapid changes in the environment and prefer familiar routines and well-established schedules rather than novel situations. Transitions and changes in routines can be upsetting and provoke anxiety. According to Prince-Hughes (2003), students with ASD often "find college to be a formidable mixture of overwhelming sights and sounds, full of change and disruption" (p. B16). See Figure 2.4 for signs of ASD among college students.

Also related to right-hemisphere differences is difficulty understanding the pragmatic elements of language: tone of voice, facial expressions, body language, and personal space. This difficulty results in problems when reading other people's emotional states or being able to understand how their perspective differs from one's own. Students on the spectrum tend to interpret language in a literal fashion. Jokes, irony, and idioms frequently cause problems in understanding. Many individuals with ASD find making eye contact painful or upsetting, so they appear indifferent or inattentive to listeners (Bennett, Tomkinson, & Miller, 2015).

Signs of ASD in College Students

In classroom
- Inappropriate social interactions
- Poor eye contact
- Poor voice intonation
- Failure to interpret tone of voice, facial expressions, or body language accurately
- Unusually strong, narrow interests (difficulty relating to general range of topics)
- Above average to superior intellect
- Literal or concrete thinking patterns
- Inflexible thinking: black/white perspectives without nuance
- Difficulty understanding others' perspectives or the concept of "audience" in writing
- High levels of general anxiety, exacerbated by novel situations or changes in routines
- Stimming: rocking, tapping, facial tics, or noises

Examples of Hyperactive-Impulsive Behavior
- Difficulty learning way around campus, directionality/accessing services
- Poor time management/balancing academic needs with personal interests
- High levels of anxiety, especially in novel situations
- Difficulty with personal finances
- Evidence of poor personal hygiene
- Difficulty with roommates
- Lack of age-appropriate friendships

Figure 2.4. Signs of ASD in college students.

These characteristics can lead to problematic classroom behaviors that may range from being argumentative and dominating a discussion to apparent apathy or disdain for peers. Outside class, they can be subject to bullying and find it painfully difficult to make and keep friends, even to the point of being perceived as stalkers when they attempt to interact with students who decline their overtures (Williams, 2018). Students with ASD may find many aspects of academic life overwhelming to the point of anxiety and agitation (e.g., following a lecture or discussion, dealing with changes in class routine, interpreting social signals from other students). Sometimes students with ASD engage in self-soothing behaviors (e.g., hand flapping, rocking, grimacing), known as stimming, to calm themselves. Others may find these behaviors distracting or irritating, which adds to the difficulty of forming appropriate peer friendships (Prince-Hughes, 2003).

66 I tend to stand back like the awkward kid in the lunch room and watch the activity rather than engage. This can be difficult for some, not all, of my family members and the attendees to accept. They are social people; therefore, it is hard for them to understand the perspective of someone who has difficulty with social interaction. I may come across as rude or inattentive when that is

really not my intention at all. However, I do not expect anyone to understand and cater to my social difficulties. Nor do I use my learning difference as a crutch. — *Megan Fabianski* 99

66 Asperger's has taken the social agent from me. Social interactions were too hard to read when I was younger so I simply stayed quiet. I am better at reading them now, but it still takes an effort to speak when I am in a group of people. ... Adults don't really understand kids or teenagers at all most of the time, especially neurotypical adults don't understand aspie kids. There is always a gap ... I look too much before I leap, get nervous about the distance and then, don't jump at all. My response to fear and stress is avoidance. — *Vanessa* 99

Referring Students for Evaluation or Services

Better understanding of students' diverse cognitive profiles should help postsecondary personnel recognize signs of LD among their students. Some students may have already approached them with an accommodations letter from campus disability services. In that case, as discussed in Chapter 1, faculty and other campus employees have a legal obligation to carry out the terms of the accommodations and to communicate with the disability services office if questions or difficulties arise.

What about signs of LD among students who have not presented accommodations letters? Should college personnel intervene if they see students struggling? Should they ask if a student has been diagnosed or received services in the past or suggest that a student seek an evaluation for a disability? Do they have an obligation to remind students of supportive services that may be available? Sensitivity to issues of identity and privacy rules that limit who is entitled to know about disability status, such as the Family Educational Rights and Privacy Act (FERPA), complicate the picture. College students who are 18 years old are legally considered adults, entitled to exercise control over who knows about their disability status. So, what are college instructors to do if they suspect a student has an eligible disability but is not accessing services that might be helpful?

The first course of action is proactive. During the first class meeting or meetings, faculty should affirm that student diversity, including cognitive diversity, is valued and invite students to talk with them privately if they have any concerns about their approach to learning. Faculty may also want to mention in a general way the availability of support through the office of student disability services and to provide contact information for the office. In addition to commenting in class, faculty should include in the syllabus a clear statement of their desire to support students with a variety of learning styles in the course.

When faculty members have concerns about particular students, they should act discreetly and privately, inviting the student to a one-on-one meeting during office hours or before or after class. At this meeting, the faculty member can objectively state observations about the student's performance and ask open-ended questions to probe the student's experiences and attitudes regarding classwork. For instance, a faculty member might observe that a student frequently hands in assignments late or that a student's written work does not seem to reflect the same caliber as contributions to class discussions. The faculty member can invite the student to comment on the observation. It can be productive to ask if the student is aware of the situation or has experienced similar issues in the past. If the student is aware and, indeed, it has occurred previously, the faculty member can follow up by asking how the student has handled it in prior situations. It is not appropriate to ask directly if a student has a disability or to suggest that this is the case, but it can be helpful to note that patterns of performance sometimes reflect an LD and that services and accommodations are available to qualified students. If the student is open to considering this possibility, a referral to disability support services is the next step. Although campuses vary widely in this regard, some schools offer diagnostic services and evaluations on campus as part of the office of disability support, and others can refer students to external evaluators nearby. If students disclose that they have had supportive services in the past, faculty members can provide information about campus disability services, such as the location of the office and related contact information, and an overview of how students can begin the process of becoming eligible for accommodations.

Conclusion

Although students with LD challenge traditional assumptions about who belongs in academia as well as how to deliver and assess instruction, institutions of higher learning cannot afford to exclude or marginalize them. Students with LD, diagnosed or not, make up an increasingly significant proportion of all entering students but often fail to thrive or even survive the rigors of academic life. Better understanding of their diverse cognitive profiles should lead to improved curricular and program design that optimizes their success and graduation rates. This process, addressed in Chapters 4 and 5, will improve access for students with LD and will benefit all students as faculty and other personnel apply the findings of contemporary research in neurobiology, cognitive psychology, and social sciences to redesign education for 21st-century learners.

CHAPTER 3
COLLEGE TRANSITION EXPERIENCES FOR STUDENTS WITH LD

The growth and challenges experienced by college students have been well documented (Astin, 1993; Pascarella & Terenzini, 1991; Tinto, 1975), and most postsecondary institutions have responded by developing programs and services to assist students in their transitions to and from college. It is important to remember that, in addition to transition challenges common to many students, students with LD may face obstacles because of the differences in the way they learn. Generalizing about the experiences of these students is problematic due to the heterogeneity of each LD as well as the likelihood that an individual has more than one learning issue or diagnosis. However, a number of theories and frameworks can be used to examine student transition, particularly as the student moves from high school to college (e.g., Chickering & Reisser, 1993; Rode & Cawthon, 2010; Schlossberg, 1981; Tinto, 1975, 2007). Although these theories provide ways for us to conceptualize transition for students, they were not designed with students with LD in mind. Overall, the topic of LD-specific transitions is under-researched (Taymans et al., 2009); however, general theories and frameworks have been used to examine the transition experiences of students with LD (see Hadley, 2011; Newman et al., 2016; Price & Patton, 2003).

One theory that offers a particularly useful framework for conceptualizing student transition that can be applied to students with LD is Schlossberg's (1981) theory of transition. This theory focuses on events or non-events and the individual's adaptation to resulting changes. A non-event is something anticipated but not realized, such as not making an athletic team in college, and can create a transition in self-image or self-esteem. In other words, specific transition experiences affect individuals and change the way they look at themselves or the world.

Chickering and Schlossberg's (1995) book, *Getting the Most Out of College*, describes the student transition experience in stages: moving in, moving through, and moving out. This chapter focuses on the challenges faced by students with LD at several critical junctures in the postsecondary experience, with Chickering and Schlossberg's categories as markers and an additional stage that anticipates the move. We start with the accommodations process, which generally begins before students start classes and is an area of confusion for many students with LD.

What is Disability Identity?

Although most individuals will experience a disability at some point in their lives given increasing life expectancy, social constructions of those with disabilities as "other" and as having deficits can profoundly impact all aspects of an individual's lived experience. As the perspectives that college students have of their own identities frequently shift throughout early adulthood, the presumption that being disabled is always the primary identity or is negative is an essentialist and simplistic view of disability identity formation. Although disability identity theories have existed for several decades, they remain controversial. Presently, a dearth of literature exists on disability identity, much less on how disability identity intersects with other identities. Still, these theories offer an interesting, albeit evolving, framework for how individuals with disabilities engage or do not engage with a single facet of their identity. The following offers an introductory exploration of how disability identity theories may aid in better understanding the transition of students with LD.

Gill's (1997) work on disability identity presented four stages of integration in identity development: (1) integrating into society as a whole, (2) integrating into a community of those with disabilities, (3) integrating sameness with differentness, and (4) coming out and integrating the self with self-presentation. According to Gill, one's identity is formed through self-awareness, interpersonal relationships, and the social sphere. The model focuses on the feelings of belonging, "coming home" to a disability community, recognizing oneself in comparison to others, and "coming out" (i.e., determining how to present oneself to others). This work has implications for both self-acceptance and advocacy for disability rights and highlights the importance of meeting students where they are in these areas. For many students with LD, the feeling of wanting to fit in with their peers is stronger than the desire to advocate for accommodations, especially in the first year.

Some students will recognize others who also struggle academically and form a bond. Jonathan Mooney and David Cole, two students with LD who met at transfer orientation at Brown University, wrote *Learning Outside the Lines*, a book about strategies for getting through college but also about the development of identities related to their LD:

> We began a mission to define ourselves for ourselves, to empower ourselves, and to use our higher education to heal old wounds, shake off old identities, and recover the lost parts of ourselves.... We took control of our education by embracing our cognitive differences, embracing alternative ways we learn, and not feeling ashamed of ourselves anymore. (2000, p. 20)

The authors were able to move beyond the comparisons to peers without disabilities to a presentation of self that is empowering.

Gibson's (2006) model of disability identity has received increased attention in student affairs due to the work of Myers and colleagues (see Myers, 2009, 2017; Myers & Bastian, 2010; Myers, Lindburg, & Nied, 2014). Gibson's model includes the passive awareness stage, typically in childhood, in which the individual has a disability but does not identify with it; the realization stage, recognizing the disability and perhaps focusing on how he or she is perceived; and the final stage of acceptance, in which the individual integrates into the world. An obvious distinction for individuals with LD, as opposed to individuals with physical disabilities or mobility issues, is that their challenges may be hidden from others and, in fact, may exist only in certain contexts, such as the academic environment. Too often, those with disabilities are confronted with the question of whether being visible is preferred to being invisible. Reaching the acceptance stage in college is not a given, so many students with LD struggle with their self-concept, whether they are struggling academically or not.

How students with LD integrate a sense of self within an academic community is difficult to assess given that the vast majority are not identifying themselves with a disability (Horowitz, Rawe, & Whitaker, 2017). However, in recent years increased attention has been given to how students incorporate specific disability labels as part of their identities. Howland and Gibavic (2013) proposed a two-tier learning disability identity model that includes a range of variables impacting one's sense of identity, including the cognitive attributes of the condition as well as the intersecting identities of each individual. The first stage includes the initial period of having a "problem" (often with the wrong name or label); getting a diagnosis; and feeling grief, relief, or both. Trying to "pass" as someone with a "problem" is also included in this stage. The second stage involves the ongoing resolution process of trying to integrate feelings of acceptance with feelings of grief. While not widely known, this model seems promising for consideration of distinct identity concerns for those with LD or other hidden disabilities for whom the acceptance phase may be much more complex.

Because one LD can be very different from another, it makes sense that individuals view themselves based on both self-concept and what they have been told by others about their disability. However, individuals may have difficulty relating to others if they do not perceive themselves as members of a distinct group. This is further complicated because terminology and labels are varied and have changed over time. For example, although many students use the labels *dyslexia* and *dyslexic*, others may avoid identifying with learning disability or use the label *learning disabled*. Furthermore, the *DSM-5* uses the label *specific learning disorder*, a term that is unlikely to be embraced by a cohort for identification purposes.

In their article on autistic identity development and college students, Gobbo and Shmulsky (2016) discussed Gibson's model of identity development. For students on the spectrum, identity development can be complicated by the medical model, which suggests autism is a disease that needs to be cured. Many individuals with ASD do not view themselves as needing to be fixed but as *neurodivergent*. College students are likely still learning about themselves, and advocating a particular position on autism may be quite difficult. Fortunately, an increasing number of individuals with ASD are, as Gill would suggest, coming out as autistic. The celebration of these individuals within the media and associated advocacy initiatives may have a positive impact on college-age students. Gobbo and Shmulsky recommended that institutions increase awareness of students with autism on campus by providing positively framed information about autistic identity and activities that celebrate the lived experience of students with ASD.

Although it is clear that more research in the area of disability identity as it relates to college students with LD is needed, rarely do individuals have singular identities. The specific ways in which different facets of identity (e.g., race, gender, sexual orientation, religion, SES, veteran status) intersect with one's disability identity are only beginning to be explored. The identity implications of having multiple disabilities have received even less attention. Among the students who received a special education in high school are individuals who have been twice marginalized based on their identities. Although research is still emerging, this twice marginalization has real implications for identity development and the transition to college.

For students of color, the fear of disclosing a disability within the context of a marginalized racial identity, combined with insufficient emphasis on transition planning and self-advocacy, may make access to appropriate accommodations even more challenging (Banks, 2014). Lower SES has also been identified as a significant barrier to a successful transition to college for those with LD (Gregg, 2007), and all students from lower SES are less likely to persist in college. Conversely, students with LD from a higher SES and who have parents with postsecondary education are more likely to succeed in college (Showers & Kinsman, 2017).

Contemplating the Move: The Accommodations Process

Students transitioning from high school to college typically are presented with a number of differences in both the academic and social environments, and those with LD may experience significant challenges in making the adjustments necessary to adapt to these new environments. These differences include the daily schedule, the type of classroom, the nature of homework, social environments, and, for many, a physical move away from the family home. At the same time, the educational and legal environments for those with LD change dramatically.

In college, although students with a diagnosis can receive accommodations for their specific learning needs, the process of obtaining accommodations is quite different from high school. Whereas in K-12 education the school is responsible for identifying students with disabilities, in postsecondary education the responsibility rests with the individual student. This responsibility requires a student to self-disclose a disability to support services professionals and provide documentation of a disability in order to receive accommodations. As part of an interactive process, disability support services (DSS) professionals must consider both the statements of a student with LD and supporting evidence in order to grant accommodations that are demonstrably linked to the specific functional limitation created by the disability. For instance, the most common accommodation, extended time on tests, is usually based on evidence that the student's disability involves slower processing of written text, with the result that it takes additional time to read, write, or both. Slower processing speed may also make a student eligible for other accommodations, such as use of a note taker, the ability to audio record a lecture, or access to an instructor's class notes. A student susceptible to distractions, often reported as a characteristic of ADHD and ASD, may be provided with the accommodation of taking a test in a quiet room with reduced distractions. In sum, these accommodations are intended to reduce barriers caused by factors that are extraneous to core academic competence so that students can access information or demonstrate academic proficiency.

> 66
> Societal attitude is the biggest barrier. I think a lot of instructors have a default belief that all students are trying to get away with something that they don't deserve, and they lump in disability with that belief. — *Chloe Corcoran, Student Advisor Alternate Format/Assistive Technology Access and Equity Services AES (formerly Disability Services for Students), University of Saskatchewan* 99

At further issue during this transition period is that parents may have difficulty letting go of the advocate role. This is understandable, as many parents have been the primary advocates for their children in school and may perceive the college environment as difficult to negotiate. As such, parents may seek to extend their roles as advocates into the college years. However, FERPA prevents college employees, including DSS professionals, from discussing student records with parents without express written consent from the students.

Since Congress amended the ADA in 2008, the accommodations process has become more student-centered and less focused on frequent updating of professional documentation. Guidelines exist for accessibility service providers to evaluate documentation, conduct constructive interviews with students, and offer accommodations specific to the disability and a student's access needs. One U.S. Department of Education study indicated that fewer than half of colleges and universities that accepted documentation for a disability would accept solely an IEP or a 504 plan to provide accommodations (Raue & Lewis, 2011), but this situation is rapidly changing. The professional organization for DSS providers, the Association of Higher Education and Disability (AHEAD), updated detailed guidelines in 2012 based on changes to the IDEA and ADA (see www.ahead.org), and this has had a positive impact on the accommodations process. Best practices in the field now allow a student's self-report to be considered a legitimate source of disability information, along with the documentation from an IEP or 504 plan from high school. Rather than focusing on the role of gatekeeper and asking for proof of disability, DSS personnel can now focus on the functional challenges that students with disabilities present and provide appropriate accommodations (Shaw, 2012).

Understanding one's legal rights as a person with a disability can be complex. However, it is important to note that acknowledging LD can still create a sense of stigma, and most students who were identified with LD in high school will not disclose their disability status in college (Horowitz et al., 2017). We do not know exactly why this is, but it is important to reflect on how colleges and universities can provide more welcoming environments for students with disabilities, reduce stigma, and demonstrate a commitment to equal access (see Chapter 6). Some students report negative experiences in which faculty do not believe they have a true disability or generalize about students with disabilities. This can discourage them from wanting to disclose in the future (Cole & Cawthon, 2015; Madaus, Scott, & McGuire, 2003). College students can have very different perspectives on whether they want to disclose a disability or not, but identifying as a person with a disability is a complex decision for many.

Moving In: Adjusting to College

Most students are both excited and nervous to enter higher education. Leaving the familiar and protective environments of home and high school, where one is known, can be daunting but is also a well-recognized rite of passage. Even the most academically prepared students intuitively understand the need to adapt to a new environment that has substantial social demands and requires adjustments to new routines, an out-of-class reading load, and different teaching styles. Many students are leaving home for the first time and are unprepared for navigating so many changes happening all at once. Although most community college and commuter students will not be living on campus, they too will experience adjustments related to increased academic demands, greater independence, and a new student cohort.

Unquestionably, the demands of college are different from those of high school, particularly if the student is living away from home. Although some students may have experienced life away from their parents (e.g., attending a boarding school, attending summer camp, traveling on an overnight school trip), generally they are accompanied by adults acting in loco parentis, responsible for structuring and monitoring day-to-day life. The transition to college marks a move away from constant adult supervision, monitoring, support, and guidance and requires life skills that many young people, with and without LD, have not yet acquired. For example, doing laundry, opening a bank account and writing checks, eating balanced and healthy meals without prompting, and picking up after themselves are all tasks that are inconsistently modeled for many first-year college students. In addition, the social situation for many students can be overwhelming, particularly if they tend to be introverted, have difficulty making friends, and, for those in residence halls, are not used to living with strangers. Although a student may have been socially successful in the presence of adult supports (e.g., parents and teachers) in the past, this does not necessarily mean they will succeed in social environments once adult supports are no longer present.

From an academic perspective, most students are used to the somewhat regular and predictable schedule of high school, even with sports, clubs, and other activities. Students with LD may have received significant guidance in adhering to a study schedule, organizing academic materials, and turning in homework. In college, students are presumed to be independent and capable of determining not only when and where to study, but for how long and how intently. Time management and organization are significant areas of difficulty for many students with ADHD or ASD, and without systems that work, these students can fall behind quickly.

> I would suggest that students register with the campus disability support office even if they think they won't use accommodations. I know often times students want a "fresh start" from high school and want to distance themselves from their disability. You can always choose not to use your accommodations, but it is so much easier to get support when the accommodations are already in place. This ensures that should students start to struggle and need the support, a plan is already in motion to support their success. — *Bridget Sullivan, Coordinator of Disability Support Services Office of Student Affairs, Cambridge College*

> I got straight A's in high school. I got into Loyola and struggled immediately. I have self-esteem issues because of my learning disability. I didn't think I could do it. I would not turn in my work. I would not hand it in even if I did it. I felt too much shame around it ... I was afraid of my professors. I didn't make it through the whole semester. — *Anna*

Social interactions sometimes prove to be obstacles for students with LD. Students on the spectrum in particular may experience challenges in the social realm, often avoiding the hub of campus activities, such as the dining hall, sports events, or the library, due to sensory overload (VanHees, Moyson, & Roeyers, 2014; see Chapter 5). Developing feelings of isolation and a sense of not belonging can happen quickly for students who are not as skilled in maneuvering social situations. Students with ADHD, in contrast, can often be very social, and this can interfere with their ability to start or complete academic work. Individuals with ADHD are statistically more prone to engage in risk-taking behaviors, including substance use, unprotected sex, and unsafe driving (Barkley, 2010; Barkley & Murphy, 2011; Shoham, Sonuga-Barke, Aloni, Yaniv, & Pollack, 2016). Fortunately, students with LD who seek out universally available supports (e.g., advising, tutoring) and disability-specific services are more likely to persist (Newman, Madaus, Lalor, & Javitz, in press).

For the students with LD who did well in secondary school, college demands may come as a shock. They may be unprepared to seek help when confronted with poor grades or increasingly difficult assignments. These students could benefit from having a close mentor, such as a faculty member, but not every student is able to find that, and many do not seek support. Faculty who have a "hidden disability" may have particularly meaningful impacts on their students if they disclose their disabilities. Seeing others acknowledge a shared perspective and serve as role models can reduce stigma for some students. Writing in *Inside Higher Ed*, Linda Kornasky, a professor with a hearing impairment, noted,

> I noticed that students with both visible and invisible disabilities exhibited a different attitude toward me and about their own identities as students with disabilities than I had perceived when I was passing as non-disabled. These students with disabilities to whom I had disclosed ... were more self-assured than my students with disabilities had been with me when I had been passing as non-disabled. (2009, ¶5)

However, disclosing a disability of any kind is complex and perhaps risky to one's career and how one is perceived by colleagues and students (see Kerschbaum, Eisenman, & Jones, 2017). Some faculty or staff may choose not to mention a diagnosis or label and instead may share their own challenges in ways that reinforce a neurodiversity model rather than a medical one.

> " I disclose the way I coach my students to disclose. I tell them first all of my qualifications for the job (which includes having been a terrible college student) and then, little by little, I speak broadly about the executive functioning challenges I have and share what I do to manage and get support. So it is not so much that I tell the students, they discover it. ... I don't ever disclose a specific diagnosis. — *Rebecca Matte, Associate Professor, Education* "

Orientation Programs

One particularly important campus program supporting the transition into college is new student orientation. Although orientations vary greatly from one institution to another, their purposes are largely the same: to help new students become familiar with campus offerings and culture while facilitating integration. In these programs, students receive information about campus policies and procedures and learn about student life (Busby, Gammel, &

Jeffcoat, 2002). For students with LD, orientation is a great opportunity to build social and academic connections. Moreover, orientation is a time when students begin to establish networks (e.g., friends, academic advisors, orientation leaders, and residential staff) that will offer support and both formal and informal guidance to students.

However, orientation may also be a difficult or anxiety-provoking experience for students with LD. They face typical college transition issues along with those associated with their LD. For example, what are the implications of no longer being covered by IDEA? What LD-related supports are available? What are the benefits of disclosing my LD and registering with disability services? Do I want to talk about my LD? Am I even still a student with LD? These questions and many more are faced by students with LD during new student orientation. Orientation professionals should be prepared to support students as they tackle these issues. Of particular importance is to ensure that from day one campus is a welcoming environment for students with disabilities. Some examples of steps that orientation professionals can take to create such an environment include

- ensuring that all programs and sessions are developed using the philosophies of universal design;
- offering sessions on disability services;
- listing disability services along with other key offices on campus that are ready to work with students;
- listing students with disabilities as an identity group when discussing campus diversity; and
- hiring qualified orientation leaders and staff with learning disabilities, ADHD, and ASD.

Frequently, new student orientation is where students with LD first engage with and learn about disability services. Although it is recommended that students with LD be aware of the disability services prior to matriculation or, better still, prior to applying to an institution (Hadley, 2007; Lalor & Madaus, 2013), this is often not the case. Increasingly, colleges and universities are offering disability-specific orientations, with some programs designed for any student with a disability and others designed for students with specific disability diagnoses. These orientation programs, although differentiating students with disabilities at the outset of their college experience and requiring early disclosure of a disability, have been a way for colleges and universities to ensure that students with disabilities get the time, attention, and support they need in order to have their unique transition concerns adequately addressed. Granted, not all students with disabilities will want or need to take part in these disability-focused orientation programs, but some may benefit and appreciate this time to form social connections, learn about disability-specific and universally available services, and adjust to new educational environments. Model orientation programs for students with disabilities can be found at the University of Connecticut and Landmark College.

Moving Through: The Sophomore Year

Increasingly, postsecondary institutions recognize that it is not solely the first-year transition that is difficult. Second-year students may experience academic challenges, disengagement, dissatisfaction with the college experience, major and career indecision, insufficient engagement with faculty, and developmental confusion (Kennedy & Upcraft, 2010). Students are more likely to drop out of school in the second year than in any other (Tobolowsky, 2008). Many students fare poorly academically in the beginning of their second year for a variety of reasons, including the adjustment to upper level courses and the expectation that they are no longer new to campus. Colleges are much more aware of the so-called *sophomore slump*, and some have focused on developing programs and initiatives to help ease the transition from the first year into the second.

As students move from their first year of college and assess their academic progress and social standing among their peers, they are sometimes asked to pick a major or career direction. Even choosing courses takes on more weight in the second year, as many students move from taking required general education courses and fulfilling other distribution requirements to deciding on interests and a major. Students at community colleges must also consider whether to continue their higher education beyond the associate degree. This is particularly important to keep in mind as data from the National Longitudinal Transition Study – 2 (NLTS2) indicate that students with learning disabilities and ASD were more likely to have been enrolled in two-year or community colleges since leaving high school (50% and 32% respectively) than four-year colleges or universities (21% and 17% respectively; Newman et al., 2011).

An analysis of the Sophomore Experiences Survey (Young, Schreiner, & McIntosh, 2015), which identified pathways to "thriving" as including campus involvement, student–faculty involvement, spirituality, and a sense of community, suggested that background characteristics of students, especially race, ethnicity, and gender, impacted outcomes. Unfortunately, disability status was not reported as a demographic variable, so little is known about the sophomore outcomes of this population of students. Given that students with LD constitute the greatest percentage of students with disabilities enrolled in higher education (51%; Raue & Lewis, 2011), reporting on disability status would provide valuable information.

Based on the results of a national survey on sophomore-year initiatives, Keup, Gahagan, and Goodwin (2010) reported that institutions were increasingly recognizing the importance of engaging second-year students and providing opportunities to assist with decision making regarding majors and career interests. Initiatives and programs cited by more than 300 institutions included career advising, leadership opportunities, and increased attention on the advising component in the sophomore year. In fact, the third iteration of the national survey in 2014 indicated that 59% of the 778 institutions had sophomore initiatives or programs (Young et al., 2015). Unfortunately, although sophomore initiatives and programs are now offered by the majority of institutions surveyed, many have not yet dedicated resources to this area or implemented strategic initiatives.

Again, a premise of our book is that well-designed programs and initiatives can benefit all students, and because the vast majority of students with LD are not identified, it is important to look at institutional improvements that will serve all students, but especially those who may have more difficulty adjusting to the many demands of college. One example of an institution engaging in efforts to better serve students in the sophomore year is Western Carolina University. Based on the idea that sophomores benefit from a sense of community and increased interaction with faculty, the university created academic-themed courses (i.e., learning communities for sophomores; Virtue, Wells, & Virtue, 2017). Although the program is not yet fully assessed, the university reports that 100% of students participating in the pilot returned the following year.

Moving Through: The Junior Year

The junior year is an important bridge for students. Community college students who enroll at a four-year institution may find themselves having to adjust to a completely new academic environment and culture in ways similar to first-year students. All students will experience heightened emphasis on college majors and potential career directions, although many will stave off decision making or proactive steps to consider life after college until the senior year. Some students may experience completely different transitions as they study abroad or engage in internship experiences, both considered high-impact practices (Kuh, 2008).

For students with LD, there may be benefits and challenges associated with experiential education. For students with ADHD, executive functioning challenges may interfere with their ability to pursue opportunities that require long-term planning, organization, and time management (e.g., completing study abroad applications, scheduling meetings with career counselors, requesting letters of recommendation for internships, developing a resume). As such, qualified students with ADHD may choose not to engage in high-impact educational experiences because they believe that preparing for them comes with insurmountable obstacles or simply that they would need to expend so much effort that it would have a negative impact their ability to complete other, more critical tasks (e.g., studying, writing papers).

Similarly, students with LD may also experience challenges associated with additional reading and writing tasks on top of their regular workloads. Students with ASD may require additional support in exploring both study abroad options and internship experiences, as meeting new people and adjusting to different physical and social environments may prove challenging. At Landmark College, the Career Connections office has designed on-campus internship experiences for students who have never been employed and who might need extra support in learning appropriate workplace behaviors before pursuing off-campus internships. Although study abroad trips can be designed with extra support, such as an additional staff member to provide help with excursions or managing logistics, it can be problematic to steer students to specific offerings when they want access to a range of experiences.

Third-year students with LD may face increased pressure to choose a career direction based on their own strengths and challenges, so career counseling is especially important. For students who have self-esteem issues and who lack strong self-advocacy skills, even considering career directions can create anxiety. As they progress in their academic programs, students will be taking more advanced courses and facing greater demands on cognitive load, time management, and organization. Ideally, students will develop the independence not only to use their strengths and experience to complete more distinguished work but also to access support when needed.

The goal of the junior year, then, might be considered a consolidation period for students, in which they optimally use a developed understanding of their individual academic and personal characteristics to consider goals for work experiences and coursework for the senior year. Although most third-year students have yet to consider the upcoming challenges of real life, there is a growing awareness that it is looming, as older friends begin to graduate and move on.

Moving On: The Senior Year

The senior year is clearly a transitional year for college students. Coursework is challenging and specific to a student's major, but it should create a focused trajectory toward graduation. Many students will be both anxious and excited about the prospect of leaving school, and what happens after graduation becomes a more pressing concern. College students can experience this period of transition as tension between the external pressures in their environments and their own developing inner voices. Becoming a confident, young adult is challenging, as external voices still dominate (Jones & Abes, 2013). For students with LD, the final year in college can bring an inordinate amount of stress and self-doubt, often due to uncertainties about the future.

Although most college students face the issue of postgraduate choice (e.g., career or graduate education), the situation for those with serious learning challenges can be magnified by a number of factors. First, students with LD have often set the goal of attaining a degree as a multiyear project with a singular focus, especially as many believe they are proving naysayers wrong or moving beyond the expectations that some teachers may have expressed in their K-12 education. Furthermore, this focus on degree attainment can limit the time students spend considering possible career and educational opportunities and preparing for their next steps. Finally, for some students with ASD, the transition from a relatively predictable college environment to the unknown can be especially stressful. Pressure to apply for jobs while trying to finish academic coursework, enjoy the social networks they have built over the previous years, and deal with the prospect of closure to the college experience can overwhelm many students. Parents, too, can sometimes exacerbate this stress as they deal with their own anxieties about their child's future.

> " In working with students with learning differences, a common challenge is getting them to activate the process at an early date. They are often consumed by coursework and their capstone projects. For those with executive functioning issues, it feels very overwhelming. Both the job search tasks and the transfer process can tend to be delayed due to the perceived immensity. The other challenge lies with finding jobs that relate to their skills and interests. They need to be willing to seek entry level positions in order to gain more professional skills. Many students today, not only those with learning differences, have little or no work experience when they graduate. It is important that they begin to accrue time in the workplace at an earlier date via summer jobs or internships. — *Jan Coplan, Director of Career Connections, Landmark College* "

Embracing the concept of high-impact practices (Kuh, 2008), many colleges have responded by increasing the focus on internship experiences in both the junior and the senior year, adding culminating experiences such as capstone courses or senior seminars, and encouraging faculty and student research collaborations. According to 2017 NSSE data, 44% of all college students participate in a senior culminating experience, with higher participation at institutions with fewer than 2,500 students. These culminating experiences can range from a discipline-specific class to a capstone project. Outcomes-based research on them is limited, but data from the 2011 NSSE suggest students who participated in any high-impact practice in the senior year—capstone, internship, or research project — reported perceived gains in work-related knowledge, especially those who participated in an internship experience. Other significant gains in the areas of integrative learning, the ability to consider real-world problems, and critical reading and writing, among others, were dependent on type of culminating experience (Kinzie, 2013). Data from the 2017 administration of the NSSE, which first included disability status in 2003, indicate that 4% of responding students (both first-year students and seniors) identified as having LD. Future research could help to identify how high-impact practices affect students with LD and more generally, any student with disabilities.

Postsecondary institutions should not only review their senior-year programs and opportunities but also attempt to assess the impact on particular groups of students at the institution over time. At Landmark College, informal assessment has resulted in the recognition that students with LD may need more scaffolding in advance of the culminating capstone course, with increased emphasis on research, synthesis, and critical problem-solving skills. Additionally, many students with LD may benefit from scaffolded work-related experiences on campus before participating in an off-campus internship. In 2016, Landmark implemented an employment readiness program, Landmark Works, for this purpose.

Employment and Career

After graduation, students with LD want to be able to transition into post-college life. For most, this transition means seeking employment. In fact, using data from the 2010 Cooperative Institutional Research Program Freshman Survey, DuPaul, Pinho, Pollack, Gormley, and Laracy (2017) found that "students with ADHD and/or [learning disabilities] placed more importance on career aspirations for attending college than did peers without disabilities" (p. 247). Unfortunately, employment rates for college graduates with disabilities are 39% lower than those of their peers without disabilities (McFarland et al., 2017). As such, opportunities to explore potential careers and develop career skills through work study, internships, and working with career services may be particularly beneficial for students with LD. Participation in career-directed activities (e.g., internships) promotes the development of job skills and has been associated with increased GPA (Astin, 1993).

Although substantial research has taken place on the topic of disability and employment at the secondary level, limited research has explored the transition from college to career for students with disabilities (Madaus, 2006). Despite the lack of research, important suggestions have been offered regarding how college and university career services programs can support this transition. Madaus (2006) conducted a survey of college graduates with learning disabilities to identify suggestions for improving college-to-career transition. Based on 170 responses, Madaus (2006) offered the following recommendations for colleges and universities:

- increase opportunities for students with learning disabilities to complete internships,
- develop mentoring programs that match students with learning disabilities with employed alumni who also have learning disabilities,
- offer coursework or seminars on learning disabilities and the transition to employment,
- provide additional education to students with learning disabilities on the Americans with Disabilities Act and the rights of employees with disabilities, and
- provide post-graduation support and follow-up for graduates transitioning to the workforce.

Graduates also suggest that students with learning disabilities develop greater self-understanding of their strengths and challenges, learn how to use this knowledge to their advantage, and learn about workplace accommodations, processes for obtaining them, and the realities of disability-related discrimination in the workplace.

As part of career services programming, it is important that professionals assist students with LD as they think through the employment search, application, and interview processes. The employment search can be exciting and anxiety-provoking for all students, but students with LD often encounter a unique set of challenges in this process. For example, writing a cover letter as a student with a language-based learning disability, interviewing as a student with ASD, and organizing and staying on task in the application process as a student with ADHD are just a few areas where students may struggle. For some students, these challenges will be familiar because they are similar to obstacles they faced in high school when they were engaged in the college search and application process. Career professionals are encouraged to have students reflect on their college search process for insight into strategies that have been successful for them in the past. Moreover, professionals can highlight how those strategies resulted in success in the past—the student got into college!

A frequent question that career professionals will undoubtedly be asked is whether a student should disclose their disability in an interview process. There is no correct answer to this question. Disclosure of LD is a personal decision and must be considered on a case-by-case basis. Some students will not want to disclose for a variety of reasons, including believing they no longer have a disability or that it is not a salient part of their identity, desire for privacy, and concerns regarding discrimination and stigmatization. Other students will want to disclose their disability to an employer if they believe it is a salient part of their identity, they may need accommodations to complete the application and interview process, or the LD may be observable (e.g., difficulty sitting still during the interview, self-stimulating behaviors). Even when students choose to disclose, they should be reminded that they can choose to disclose only certain aspects of the disability and keep other aspects private. Tracie DeFreitas (2018) of the Job Accommodation Network (JAN) noted that individuals with disabilities should be thoughtful about when and to whom they disclose their disability. Disclosing too early or too late can be problematic. To be clear, some—but certainly not all—employers and members of search committees will discriminate based on disability status. In fact, 26,838 charges of disability discrimination were filed with the Equal Employment Opportunity Commission in fiscal year 2017, and this number appears to be increasing with each passing year (U.S. Equal Employment Opportunity Commission, n.d.). Thus, unless an accommodation is needed during the pre-employment phase, it may be worth waiting to disclose a disability until after being hired and any negotiations have been completed. It will be important for students to consider when the best time will be, and career counselors can assist students with navigating this process. Career counselors and students with disabilities preparing for employment are encouraged to make use of the wealth of resources offered on the JAN website (https://askjan.org/).

Conclusion

Higher education, by its very nature, consists of transitions. Although the transition to college and the transition from college tend to be marked by pomp and circumstance, less celebrated transitions that can have a significant impact on students with LD can be found at various junctures. Though all college students can be said to be moving through stages of development into a more secure sense of independence and adulthood, students with LD may face particular challenges. At each stage of transition, students with LD encounter new obstacles that they must consider. Understanding these transition obstacles and working proactively to support students with LD as they meet them should be a goal of all educators. Simply piling on activities and opportunities for students is not necessarily effective, and most educators recognize that various factors are at work not only in students' engagement with college life and their academic courses but also in the development of a range of skills that better prepare them for the challenges of college and beyond (see Chapter 4). Postsecondary institutions can develop appropriate programs and initiatives by assessing student outcomes throughout the college experience and the students' own perspective on these outcomes.

CHAPTER 4
SUPPORTING STUDENTS WITH LD IN THE CLASSROOM

What do instructional and administrative personnel need to know in order to optimize success for students with LD as they enter postsecondary education? This chapter focuses on classroom approaches, supports, and strategies that promote academic success for these students, highlighting their potential contributions to diversity within the academic community. We begin with an overview of cognitive load theory, which helps educators understand and address how individual cognitive differences impact the learning process. Next, beneficial classroom practices for each cognitive profile discussed in Chapter 2 (i.e., dyslexia, dyscalculia, attention-deficit/hyperactivity disorder, and autism spectrum disorder) are described. Finally, we examine how to support students in online courses and advocate a universal design (UD) approach to instruction that benefits all students, including those with LD.

Beyond Accommodations

Chapter 1 includes a review of the legally mandated accommodations model for supporting students with LD, which currently guides practice in postsecondary institutions across the United States and in many countries internationally. Accommodations are designed to level the playing field for students with LD, but as noted earlier, the process for acquiring the right to accommodations can be arduous and stigmatizing. Furthermore, as suggested in the following sections, accommodations address only a few of the challenges that students with LD typically encounter in the classroom.

Colleges and universities that hope to serve and retain not only students identified with LD but also the large numbers of students who do not disclose and who were never diagnosed with disabilities need to go beyond offering accommodations. They need to anticipate the challenges faced by students with diverse cognitive profiles and proactively build accessibility into curricular and program structures. The outcome of such an approach is a more welcoming environment for those who learn differently.

Considering Cognitive Load

Cognitive load theory (CLT) provides a framework for understanding how the range of difficulties experienced by students with LD can interfere with their ability to achieve academic success comparable to that of their neurotypical peers. The premise of CLT is that human brains have limited capacity to hold and process discrete chunks of information.

Cognitive scientists call this capacity *working memory* or the *cognitive workspace*, sometimes likened to a workbench or countertop.

For most learners, working memory is the major bottleneck when it comes to processing (i.e., receiving or expressing) new information. Working memory tends to have limited capacity (once thought to be seven discrete items but more recently, closer to four) and is significantly impacted by individual variations in language processing and executive function (EF) (Cowan, 2010). CLT provides a useful framework for identifying and modifying instructional elements that impede learning by overwhelming students' working memory capacity, thus making learning activities accessible to a wider range of individuals. Theorists have identified at least two kinds of cognitive load (Sweller, 2010):

- **Extraneous load** is any element of cognitive processing that is not a core part of the current learning task. Often this load is imposed by the instructional approach used to teach or test the content rather than the task itself. Extraneous load could potentially be removed or replaced without impacting the essential goals of the task. For example, students in a biology lab learning about the anatomy of a frog could either read a description or perform a dissection in a lab. For students with reading difficulties, the former would impose a far higher extraneous load than the latter, but the learning goal in both cases remains the same.

- **Intrinsic load** refers to cognitive processing that is a core element of a learning task and cannot be changed without altering the learning goals. This load can be thought of as the productive mental effort in which a student engages to reach a desired learning outcome. For example, instructors can present an algebraic task either as a word problem or with figures, formulas, and tables. In either case, students will expend the same mental effort to solve the problem (i.e., the intrinsic load), but the format itself will pose different levels of extraneous load to students of varying cognitive profiles.

In addition to clarifying how specific cognitive deficits translate into academic difficulty, CLT offers educators insights into how to structure activities, assignments, and assessments in order to optimize learning for students of all cognitive profiles. It identifies unintended barriers that arise when assignments are created and formatted without regard to students' cognitive diversity. Educators who take cognitive load into account can offer students options in how they access content or express knowledge. This empowers students to select options that minimize the extraneous load caused by their particular cognitive profiles without changing the intrinsic nature of the task. For example, for the algebraic task mentioned previously, instructors might offer students options such as accessing the task as a word problem or as a data chart or explaining their solution in a paragraph or in a diagram.

Serving Students With Specific Cognitive Profiles

Although much of the UD literature advocates flexibility and options in delivering content and assessing learning, it is critical for instructors to know which options actually enhance learning for students with diverse cognitive profiles. Having more options does not necessarily translate into better educational outcomes. In fact, there is a cognitive cost to offering options, as students expend mental effort in selecting among them. Therefore, understanding the kinds of options that improve academic success for students with specific types of LD is critical. In many cases, approaches designed to support one profile of student will be beneficial to a wider range of learners.

Serving Students with Language-Based Learning Disabilities

Like fish who are unaware that they are swimming in water, educators take for granted the medium of language, which permeates almost all academic learning. However, for students with language-based learning disabilities, language itself—the "medium of the message"—can present a barrier to successful learning. When designing activities and assignments, instructors do well to consider cognitive load factors, such as the accuracy, speed, and efficiency with which students process language, in addition to the intrinsic elements of the learning task. This section looks at how to help students navigate the oral and print language elements of the classroom experience, even in specialized, nonlinguistic courses such as mathematics, music, and visual arts.

Reading texts. The digital revolution has altered the academic landscape for everyone, but perhaps most dramatically for individuals with print-based difficulties, including students who are blind, visually impaired, or dyslexic as well as students disadvantaged by not being native speakers of the dominant language. Personal computing has transformed the way scholars interact with text. For many students with LD, these developments have been life-changing, making academic success possible where it may have been out of reach or, at the least, intensely laborious and time consuming in the past.

Arguably, the single most beneficial support for students with dyslexia and other language-based LDs is for texts to be available digitally, which allows students to modify print formatting to enhance reading efficiency. Research has shown that many students with dyslexia find larger, sans serif fonts to be more accessible, especially when formatted with widely spaced lines in skinny columns that increase the amount of white space on a page (Eide, 2015; Schneps, Thomson, Chen, Sonnert, & Pomplun, 2013). Though the research is controversial, some students report improved reading when they can alter the color of the font or the page, increasing the contrast between text and background or reducing glare (Uccula, Enna, & Mulatti, 2014). Additionally, digital text offers instant access to dictionary, thesaurus, and other reference tools, bypassing the cumbersome challenge of consulting a second text or the need for automatic alphabetizing skills.

Perhaps most important, digital text affords the option of having the text spoken aloud when used in conjunction with a text-to-speech (TTS) reader. Text can be read aloud word by word or continuously, at a pace that allows the reader to comprehend. The variability of pacing is important because some dense texts need to be processed slowly, whereas others might be processed very quickly (e.g., passages with abundant examples). The benefits of hearing text, and especially simultaneous hearing and reading, are well documented, especially for students with LD. Individuals with dyslexia and ADHD show improved reading speed, comprehension, and stamina when text is heard as well as seen (Hecker et al., 2002). This makes it possible for students to navigate the much heavier reading load they typically encounter when they transition to college. Digital text also makes text annotation easier and more efficient. Students can highlight in multiple colors and add a variety of notes, including voice notes. Many TTS tools allow readers to extract notes and highlights into separate files, which can be used as study guides or incorporated into critical essays. In addition, digital text can be converted to MP3 files so students can listen on their phones while commuting to school.

Until recently, TTS was costly and specialized, but now it is built into most personal computers, tablets, and smartphones. Today students with and without disabilities use TTS technology to access books, periodicals, websites, text messages, and pretty much any other form of digital text. Its ubiquity has nearly erased the stigma of using TTS and has made it accessible to all students, not just those who request and qualify for accommodations. Table 4.1 highlights a variety of digital tools for supporting reading and writing.

What does this mean for instructors and academic program planners? In order for all students to access these benefits, texts need to be available in digital formats. Increasingly, standard college texts and course packs are available this way, but instructors should consider this when selecting readings. Ideally, in-class handouts and additional readings should be available digitally and posted on a course website for convenient access. When items are to be read in class, instructors should allow enough time for slower readers to process the text, providing supplementary activities to engage faster readers without penalizing those who take longer. Although some logistical challenges may arise, tests and exams should also be available digitally, eliminating the need for readers or scribes, which are sometimes mandated as accommodations for students with print-based disabilities.

Table 4.1
Technology Tools for Reading and Writing

Type of Tool	Purpose	Examples
Text-to-speech	Reads text out loud, with variable speeds and voices to promote fluency, comprehension, attention, and reading stamina	Kurzweil Read & Write (TextHelp) Voice Dream Reader (for tablets) Built-in accessibility tools on Macs and PCs
Voice recognition	Transcribes speech into digital text to bypass keyboarding or handwriting difficulty and spelling issues	Dragon Built-in accessibility tools on Macs and PCs
Graphic organizers	Creates mind maps to generate and organize ideas, visually showing relationships among concepts. Supports both notetaking and organizing ideas for writing	Inspiration XMind Popplet

Academic writing. Because students with LD may require additional time for writing as well as reading, in-class writing assignments should be scheduled so that they do not penalize students who are slower to process text. At the basic level of transcription, handwriting and spelling difficulties impose predictable barriers for many students with language-based disabilities. Some students with LD also experience word retrieval difficulty, making fluent written expression problematic. Cumulative difficulties with written expression predictably foster deep-seated anxiety in many students when it is time to write.

> I experience severe anxiety when trying to write, fear of what my teachers will say to me, fear of how they will treat me because I can't write the way they want or when they want, and I struggle to find a voice inside myself telling me I am a competent writer. I procrastinate out of fear and spiral into a depression from which writing does not flow because a bear named Anxiety is sitting on my chest. … More emphasis in higher education could go towards helping students understand how their emotions and anxiety factor into their writing with solutions to manage time, set reasonable expectations, and understand the role of emotions in writing. — *Rory* **99**

For students who disclose a print-based disability and qualify for accommodations, these core difficulties are often addressed by allowing additional time for composing and offering the use of a laptop or tablet. These practices could be offered to other students without compromising academic integrity. After all, most professionals are now required to file notes and reports electronically and, unless speed of production is a critical feature of performance, on a flexible timetable. Rather than singling out specific students preferentially, allowing access to a laptop or tablet could be a standard part of classroom practice under a UD approach that offers options for accessing information and expressing knowledge based on student preferences.

Anyone who has produced academic text digitally can appreciate the many advantages of word processing as compared to writing by hand (e.g., speed of transcription, ease of editing and revising, ease of saving and sharing documents, access to spell- and grammar-checking). Although clearly beneficial for most students, access to word processing for in- and out-of-class writing, including quizzes, tests, and exams, may mean the difference between academic success and failure for students with dyslexia and attention difficulties (Batorowicz, Missiuna, & Pollock, 2012; MacArthur, 2009; Peterson-Karlan, 2011).

In addition to basic word processing tools, laptops and tablets offer some specialized advantages over writing by hand. Many students who struggle to organize their thoughts on the page benefit from beginning the composing process using graphic organizers, such as mind maps and spider webs, which not only capture ideas visually but also show connections between ideas spatially (Learning Disabilities Association of America, n.d.b). Higher quality graphic organizer tools, such as Inspiration™ software, easily convert visual arrays into an outline format that can flexibly be re-sequenced by the writer.

Another beneficial tool for composing is voice recognition software, which bypasses the challenges of handwriting, keyboarding, and spelling by transcribing text directly from spoken language. Many students, not just those with LD, freeze or go blank when asked to transfer thoughts from their heads to the written page. If they can articulate ideas orally to produce a rough draft that can be reorganized and revised to follow academic conventions, they may experience greater success in the writing process. Oral writing processes do not have to take place at a desk; students can dictate from wherever they have access to the technology—even while walking, running, and painting, which often encourages the free flow of ideas (Dunn, 2001; Hecker, 1997).

Providing templates or structured outlines for writing assignments clarifies expectations concerning scope, sequence, and depth of coverage that are more useful than a suggested number of words or pages (see Figure 4.1). Furthermore, if academic writing is not a core competency associated with a course, instructors can offer alternatives to written assignments designed to assess content knowledge. For example, oral presentations, demonstrations, diagrams and charts, and graphic or video arrays are a few of the many ways students might express their command of a topic.

Basic Essay Structure

| Introduction | **Introductory Information** |
| | Thesis Statement |

Body Paragraphys	**Topic Sentence**
	Supporting Details
	Topic Sentence
	Supporting Details
	Topic Sentence
	Supporting Details

| Conclusion | Summary of the main points and your closing remarks. Leave the reader thinking. |

Figure 4.1. Basic essay template (used with permission of author Linda Hecker).

Oral language and lectures: Note-taking. Many students with dyslexia encounter difficulties primarily with print, but a significant minority also experience difficulty processing oral language fast enough to keep up with classroom lectures and discussions (Bishop & Snowling, 2004). These individuals may have trouble participating appropriately in discussions, debates, and small-group work that often characterize classroom experiences.

They are likely to have particular difficulty taking notes, a skill that involves simultaneous processing of receptive (i.e., hearing) and expressive (i.e., writing) language. This is the primary reason that assigning a student a note taker or allowing access to a professor's lecture notes is a common accommodation granted by disability service offices. However, these are imperfect solutions because (a) the notes may be difficult to understand due to their organization and style and (b) the recipient is deprived of the opportunity to process information deeply. For this reason, students receiving notes are often encouraged to review and synthesize them with what they heard or wrote in class, but this imposes additional work on the student. Furthermore, being singled out to receive someone else's notes can be uncomfortable for many students, who may fear that they will be perceived by peers as receiving unfair advantages.

Learning how to take and use notes efficiently is a lifelong learning skill that is especially critical for at-risk students as they transition to the increased rigors of college courses. Some colleges offer note-taking workshops specifically for students who identify as LD, but because the majority of students will not disclose disabilities, note-taking instruction is sometimes built into first-year seminars or other introductory classes taken in the first semester. Such instruction benefits those with LD, a range of underprepared students who never developed note-taking skills, and students who are not native English speakers. Landmark College's Master Notebook System is a classroom-tested approach originally developed for dyslexic high school students (Hecker & Fein, 2014). Although it initially teaches a two-column note-taking system based on the classic book, *How to Study in College* (Pauk & Owens, 2014), it is easily adaptable to many systems of capturing information, whether transcribed by hand or keyboarding. This system provides students with a step-by-step process for reviewing and annotating their notes on a regular basis (preferably daily) rather than just right before tests and exams. Review includes a series of elaborative rehearsal techniques, such as highlighting key ideas and vocabulary and adding questions, visuals, and summaries to support deeper processing of the content as the course proceeds. This system of iterative revision can also be applied to notes supplied by a note taker or instructor, in order to clarify and facilitate retention of information.

Instructors in first-year courses that do not include explicit instruction in fundamentals of note taking can nevertheless support high-quality note taking by discussing discipline-specific challenges and modeling appropriate organizational structures through their use of organized black/whiteboard presentations and in-class handouts.

Supporting Students with Dyscalculia

Students with dyscalculia are not likely to need institutional support for their challenges, except in mathematics courses and some science courses that rely heavily on math competence. The first line of support for students with dyscalculia may be to select courses that minimize their challenges. In some circumstances, colleges may elect to grant waivers from math courses, especially in the first year, or offer a course substitution such as Math Concepts or Statistics for a more traditional requirement like College Algebra or Calculus. It is also recommended that students with dyscalculia take math classes on a pass/fail basis so that their disabilities do not have a disproportionately negative impact on their GPAs.

Students with dyscalculia are likely to perform poorly in large, fast-paced lecture courses. If available, a computer-based, self-paced math course that offers ample clear illustrations, examples of procedures, and easy access to terms and definitions may be more conducive to success (Dyscalculia.org, n.d.a). When it is not appropriate to provide a waiver or course substitution, permission (and encouragement) to use a calculator is probably the accommodation with the most immediate benefit for students with dyscalculia because they may be able to grasp higher math concepts despite difficulty with basic calculations. Additional time to complete tests is an appropriate low-cost, low-tech accommodation. Other helpful strategies include using graph paper to align columns of figures and colored pencils to differentiate kinds of problems or highlight the type of operation (e.g., addition or multiplication).

For students who have difficulty grasping math concepts, beneficial tools include visual diagrams, illustrations, and manipulatives such as geo-boards, tokens, and graphing models (Learning Disabilities Association of America, n.d.a). Math disability expert Mahesh Sharma (n.d.) suggested a pedagogically sound sequence for introducing math concepts and problem types that includes

- using language to talk about the key concepts;
- introducing the general principle or law;
- letting students investigate aspects of the principle using concrete materials, such as using manipulatives to discover proof of the concepts;
- giving many specific examples using concrete materials;
- having students talk about their findings and understandings;
- explicitly demonstrating how individual student discoveries support or give examples of the general concept; and
- having students restate the general principle and teach it to one another.

Supporting Students With ADHD and Executive Function Challenges

Students with ADHD and EF difficulties face more global challenges in academia than their peers who have dyslexia, whose difficulties cluster around reading and writing. Cognitive load factors for students with ADHD relate to their difficulty in activating and sustaining focus; screening out distractions; and planning, organizing, and completing academic tasks. Students with ADHD may appear to have strong-to-outstanding skills in reading, writing, discussing, and calculating but fail to hand in assignments on due dates or show up for class on a regular basis. They may be able to create detailed plans for completing long-range writing projects but then fail to meet one checkpoint after the next. As Barkley (2004) remarked about students with EF challenges, "It's not that they don't *know how*; it's just that they don't *do it*" (emphasis added). In addition, students may be acutely self-conscious about the gap between their potential and their performance, and they may experience overwhelming shame and self-blame, falling into unproductive patterns of denial and avoidance. Often, they start a new program or semester with enormous energy and optimism, only to fall helplessly behind, withdrawing sometime between midterms and finals.

Importantly, it is not just students with diagnosed ADHD who experience these difficulties. Because the parts of the brain that control EF are the last to mature, these behaviors may characterize many entering students at least some of the time. Furthermore, individuals with ADHD, ASD, and other related neurodevelopmental syndromes, whether diagnosed or not, often show a developmental lag, so that they perform at approximately two-thirds the maturity level of their chronological peers, according to Barkley (2004). This means they may not be prepared to navigate the demands typically placed on first-year students, both academically and socially. Behaviors that are often attributed to lack of motivation, character defects, or poor parenting in reality may be better explained by examining the brain function and structure in these individuals.

The accommodations model has been slow to adapt to the evolving understanding of ADHD as a disorder of executive functioning. Although college students who have disclosed and documented a diagnosis of ADHD are eligible to receive accommodations, often those accommodations address only a few of their difficulties. Typical accommodations include extended time on tests (usually "time and a half"), testing in a separate and quiet location, access to note takers, and permission to record lectures. However, extended time on tests provides no benefit if students have not learned efficient strategies for reviewing and revising their work or if they have a co-occurring learning disability such as dyslexia that involves slower processing of language. Likewise, without a protocol for reviewing and personalizing notes from a note taker or a recording, students with ADHD do not benefit much from note-taking accommodations. Furthermore, these accommodations do not address the majority of substantive issues caused by poor executive functioning.

EF-Friendly Classroom

How can instructors optimize academic success for students with these seemingly intractable difficulties in planning, prioritizing, organizing, and, especially, completing work? Landmark College has developed a multipoint framework for what it calls the EF-friendly classroom. Keeping in mind that entering college students of all cognitive profiles face increased challenges in self-regulation at the very time when their typical support systems (e.g., parents, high school teachers) are no longer available, the EF-friendly classroom scaffolds the classroom experience for a range of diverse learners. Strategies for creating an inclusive environment for those who experience EF difficulties include the following:

- understanding the impact of EF on performance,
- bringing explicit attention to EF tasks and skills needed for success,
- creating routines,
- providing steps and guidelines to meet expectations,
- using deadlines strategically, and
- adopting a coaching mindset.

We address each of these strategies in more depth in this section.

The impact of EF on performance. Viewing EF difficulties as cognitive challenges rather than personality defects helps educators partner with students to address difficulties by taking a problem-solving approach. Educators also benefit from having an objective framework and common language they can use when talking about these issues with students.

One model of EF that is particularly useful when thinking about classroom impacts of ADHD was developed by Dr. Thomas E. Brown (Brown Clinic, n.d.; see Figure 4.2) who identified six areas of EF, which may work singly or in various combinations to impact performance. It is possible to understand the wide variability of student behaviors by considering which of the six areas have the strongest influence on an individual's behaviors and targeting one or two areas to prioritize for strategic interventions. It helps to shift the discussion from a global difficulty to a specific cognitive issue that can be addressed through a problem-solving approach. Table 4.2 shows Brown's definition of each area along with the challenges students with EF limitations might experience when completing long-range writing assignments.

EF tasks and skills needed for success. Brown's model serves as a planning tool for designing instruction that achieves intended outcomes without unfairly disadvantaging students of a particular cognitive profile. It reminds instructors to consider the contribution of EF to the extraneous cognitive load of an assignment or assessment, anticipating difficulties that students may face beyond those intrinsic to the task. For instance, it may prompt instructors to address EF issues proactively by providing students with a model for how to break a long-range writing assignment into incremental steps or direct them to a digital assignment planner such iStudiezPro™ (istudentpro.com/) or the University of Minnesota's free Online Assignment Calculator (https://www.lib.umn.edu/ac/). It also reminds instructors of students' limited capacity for sustaining focus on new information over the course of a class lecture. Although students' ability to concentrate is highly variable, a good rule of thumb based on current understanding of working memory is to present lecture-formatted information in relatively short chunks of no more than 20 minutes (i.e., about the length of a TED talk) before switching to an activity that actively engages students in talking, writing about, or applying the concepts just presented (Ebert-May, Brewer, & Allred, 1997).

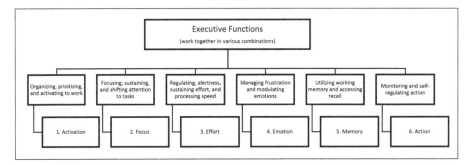

Figure 4.2. Executive functions impaired in ADD/ADHD. From "The Brown Model of ADD/ADHD" by T. E. Brown, http://www.brownadhdclinic.com/add-adhd-model/. Reprinted with permission.

Sharing insights with students about the myriad EF challenges associated with most academic tasks helps them improve their ability to self-regulate by promoting metacognition, a foundational skill for student success. Helping students anticipate and plan for difficulties is one of the beneficial practices instructors can build into courses, especially for newly entering college students (Nilson & Zimmerman, 2013). For the long-range writing project, for example, instructors can ask students to anticipate difficulties they may have completing it on time and to devise a work plan that includes not only Plan A but also a Plan B as a contingency for unanticipated obstacles and interruptions. Students can also discuss the challenges of sustaining effort over the course of the assignment and how they might access out-of-class support from a campus writing center, a student-created study group, or faculty office hours.

Giving students language to discuss EF challenges helps them move from self-blame to a problem-solving approach and to realize that they are not alone in facing these difficulties. These insights help students develop higher levels of self-determination and agency and an internal locus of control, all of which are frequently diminished in students with ADHD or EF difficulties (Nilson & Zimmerman, 2013).

Table 4.2

Identifying Executive Function Challenges Associated With a Long-Range Writing Assignment

Executive function	Definition	Associated challenges
Activation	Planning how to approach the task, including when and where to begin; breaking large tasks into incremental steps; actually getting started on the task(s) at the appointed time	Breaking the writing project into subtasks; scheduling each task; initiating tasks at appointed times (avoiding procrastination)
Focus	Sustaining concentration and focus on the task until it's completed	Sustaining concentration at each designated writing session and throughout entire writing process
Effort	Maintaining consistent level of effort and pacing in each session and throughout the entire process; not falling asleep at the wheel; not working too slowly (perseverating on steps) or too quickly; not rushing through essential tasks in order to be done	Working at efficient pace at each session; not running out of gas or rushing toward the end
Emotion	Tamping down negative feelings, including frustration and anxiety; setting aside anger, sadness, or fear arising from other life circumstances	Setting aside negative feelings about writing based on prior difficulties or current life events
Memory	Allocating working memory to task at hand; accessing relevant information from long-term memory	Keeping in mind the big picture of the assignment (i.e., purpose, audience) while organizing ideas; recalling rules and conventions, such as spelling, punctuation, and citations, while thinking about content
Action	Monitoring performance during the entire task; adjusting work plans when difficulties arise or circumstances change	Reviewing work in progress; adjusting work schedule when circumstances change; having a Plan B if Plan A does not work out

Note. Definitions of executive function from "The Brown Model of ADD/ADHD" by T. E. Brown, http://www.brownadhdclinic.com/add-adhd-model/. Reprinted with permission.

Routines. Creating class routines around common procedures for entering and leaving the classroom (e.g., warm-up activities, stowing electronic devices, taking out and putting away lab equipment), preparing for activities, taking tests, handing in assignments, and so on, provides a supportive structure that benefits all students, but particularly those with ADHD and other EF challenges. When a procedure is a habit, it does not require conscious effort to execute, freeing up cognitive work space to focus on the intrinsic cognitive load elements of a task. These routines also set a positive classroom tone that places value on productivity and reduces student anxiety about standards and expectations.

Clear expectations. Along with routines, clear and explicit expectations for class behavior and assignment completion help reduce students' anxiety about their ability to participate successfully and complete tasks. Just as talking with students about EF challenges can deepen their metacognitive understanding and self-regulation, holding a frank discussion about classroom behavioral standards in the early days of a course can contribute positively to building a supportive community of learners. Discussing students' ideas for how a classroom functions is a good entry point for talking about cognitive diversity while setting standards for participation. At Landmark College, most semester-long courses begin with a discussion in which students determine the rules for classroom behavior and define what they mean by respect and fairness. These rules are often posted on the board or on the walls throughout the semester to cue students about expectations, and students are quick to remind one another of them when lapses occur, relieving instructors of some of the burden of managing classroom decorum. Landmark College first-year faculty have renamed these procedures Professional Behavior Guidelines instead of Classroom Participation Expectations to emphasize common standards for behavior shared by the classroom and the workplace.

Explicitly previewing expectations for assignments, not just expectations of length but also of depth and range of content, can reduce student anxiety and assist students at the activation stage by providing a clear road map or sequence of steps to guide their work (Hill, 2016). Students appreciate rubrics as explicit, objective guides to faculty expectations (Reddy & Andrade, 2010). Instructors can amplify the benefits of rubrics by (a) designing classroom activities that offer students practice in applying rubric criteria to example work and (b) discussing the extent to which the examined work meets or fails to meet the criteria. It is especially helpful for students to examine examples of student work of varying quality (e.g., papers that earned a C as well as those that earned an A).

Templates serve a similar function of clarifying expectations by specifying the required elements, formats, and organization. These can take the form of a skeleton outline or a graphic organizer, such as the basic essay format depicted in Figure 4.1.

Strategic deadlines. Procrastination and failure to complete assignments are hallmarks of EF difficulty in the classroom. Empathetic instructors may be inclined to extend deadlines for students who struggle with these issues, but paradoxically, it is more helpful to increase the frequency of deadlines. Giving students extended time is the equivalent of giving them enough rope to hang themselves. Imminent deadlines provide the extra stimulus that drives people into action; that is why students with ADHD and EF difficulties tend to put off starting projects until the night before they are due. Firm deadlines, with point penalties for lateness, provide an extra level of accountability for students who tend to procrastinate. If students approach an instructor requesting an extension, it may be more beneficial to negotiate a series of interim deadlines for segments of the paper or project than to grant additional time for the final product.

A coaching mindset. Executive function coaching is one of the most effective supports for college students with ADHD or EF difficulties (Parker & Boutelle, 2009). Instructors can support the growth of student self-determination and self-regulation by using coaching techniques in their interactions with students. The core coaching technique is the use of open-ended, nonjudgmental questioning to encourage students to draw on their internal resources to prioritize concerns and develop strategies to address them. Coaching shifts the instructor–student dialogue from one in which instructors define problems and suggest solutions (e.g., "I think you should…") to one in which they ask students curious questions about what's important to them, what gets in the way of fulfilling their goals, and what solutions might be available to them. It moves students toward creating a Plan A for action that specifies a time and place for carrying out tasks as well as a Plan B for the inevitable contingencies that interfere with Plan A. This model is discussed more fully in Chapter 6.

Supporting Students With Autism Spectrum Disorder (ASD)

Individuals with ASD constitute the most recent wave of students with distinct cognitive profiles to arrive on campus—are one of the fastest-growing subgroups of students with disabilities at postsecondary institutions (HEATH Resource Center, n.d.). Many of the difficulties encountered by students with ASD fall outside the classroom experience and are covered in Chapter 5. However, the academic experience for these students can also be problematic in many ways. Students with ASD are perhaps the most likely to challenge faculty and peer expectations about appropriate college classroom behavior. The social communication difficulties that characterize many students with ASD may disrupt lectures and discussions and tax faculty's ability to maintain a productive classroom environment. These difficulties may include poor eye contact; attempts to monopolize conversation while denigrating the abilities of classmates; tangential responses to questions that circle back to the student's unusually strong but narrow area(s) of expertise; and self-stimulating behaviors such as rocking, tapping, hand flapping, or playing with stress toys (Shmulsky & Gobbo, 2013). As noted by Wheeler,

> the observable behaviors of students on the autism spectrum may make them appear inattentive, bored, rude, defiant or possibly even on drugs. Ritualistic or repetitive behaviors, an attachment to incongruous objects and additional unusual communication and social skills (especially under stress) can make some of these students seem odd and bring unwanted attention to them. (Wheeler, n.d., ¶2)

Less often discussed, but nevertheless significant, are difficulties with critical thinking. Students with ASD, though often highly intelligent, may struggle with abstract and critical thinking and may approach complex concepts less flexibly than neurotypical peers. Frequently, students with ASD are characterized as thinking in black-and-white dichotomies, rather than shades of difference. Often detail oriented and possessing strong rote memory, students with ASD may find it difficult to summarize, synthesize, and apply abstract concepts. A characteristic common to many students with ASD is that they tend to interpret language (e.g., humor, sarcasm, irony) literally. This can prove problematic in the classroom as well as in social situations. Difficulty in understanding diverse perspectives and anticipating the needs of an audience or reader impacts their ability to participate appropriately in discussions and debates and to complete written assignments at a postsecondary level (Gobbo & Shmulsky, 2014).

Beyond Accommodations for Students with ASD

Many of the accommodations commonly available to students with ASD who register with disability services offices are similar to those offered to students with dyslexia or ADHD. A representative listing from City College of New York includes the following:

- extended time on exams;
- alternative format tests;
- distraction-reduced testing space;
- reduced course load;
- extended time on assignments; and
- access to class notes, a note taker, or use of a tape recorder for lectures (CUNY Council on Student Disability Issues, 2014).

These accommodations address a few of the challenges experienced by students with ASD; however, they fail to address the social communications challenges that may cause the most difficulty. Needless to say, these accommodations are not available to the large number of students with ASD who decide not to register with disability services. Strategies for moving beyond these basic accommodations and creating a more inclusive learning environment for students with ASD are the focus of the rest of this section.

Communication: Lectures and discussions. Faculty members can forestall some of the predictable communication difficulties experienced by students with ASD by striving to be "clear, concise, concrete and logical when communicating" (Wheeler, n.d., ¶8). Faculty are encouraged to avoid excessive use of figurative language, idioms, sarcasm, and irony. Clarity regarding expectations about how assignments are to be formatted and when they are to be completed is helpful to all students, particularly those with ASD, who often experience anxiety about their performance. Common methods for offering clarity around assignments include templates and rubrics. Even with explicit guidelines, students on the spectrum may express confusion or anxiety about expectations and may continue to ask for further clarification.

Similarly, students with ASD may exhibit weak understanding of the unspoken rules for classroom behaviors, especially around student-to-student interactions. They sometimes tend to dominate discussions with questions or statements of their own opinions, and they may appear inflexible about accepting perspectives and opinions different from their own (Shmulsky & Gobbo, 2013). As already suggested for students with ADHD, it may be helpful to post in the classroom a student-generated set of professional behaviors that spells out what is meant by respect and specifies protocols about verbal interchanges (e.g., Should students raise their hands to speak? Are they expected to paraphrase what someone has said before adding their own opinions?).

For students who consistently violate established classroom decorum, faculty members may need to set individual expectations with explicit guidelines for behavior. To ensure student privacy, the faculty member should consider meeting with a student one-to-one during office hours. Strategies that may prove useful for both students and professors include providing specific limits to the number of questions a student may ask, using a record-keeping tool for students to track themselves, and developing a discreet cueing system to remind students when they have exceeded their specified limits (e.g., standing near the student's seat or signaling with a predetermined hand gesture).

Social skills/collaborations. Face-to-face classes include a social dimension that may raise difficulties for students with ASD, such as making eye contact or recognizing the unwritten rules of reciprocal conversation (e.g., active listening, taking turns speaking, and staying on topic). Many individuals with ASD have extreme social anxiety that is expressed in difficulty relating to others, particularly when interacting in pairs or small groups. Students with ASD may misinterpret facial expressions and other nonverbal cues, due in part to heightened anxiety, and may be quicker to take offense at perceived, although unintended, put-downs. In addition, students with ASD may offer pointedly candid opinions about peers, minus tact or compassion.

It is helpful for instructors (and peers) to honor a student's chosen level of eye contact without judgment. When it comes to collaborations or group work, instructors should assist in the formation and monitoring of pairs or groups of students to ensure the proper inclusion of students with an ASD diagnosis. Group assignments benefit from clearly stated lists of tasks and expected outcomes, as well as specific assigned roles, such as timekeeper, moderator, recorder, or spokesperson.

Sensory overload. Students with ASD may be highly sensitive to levels of visual, auditory, and tactile stimulation that others can ignore (e.g., fluorescent lights, humming

LCD projectors or ventilation systems, room temperature fluctuations). Sometimes students with ASD react to these stimuli by abruptly leaving class without explanation. It is helpful for faculty members to discuss options with students privately in advance of an actual meltdown, so that they can anticipate potential sensory triggers and develop escape plans should a student experience sensory overload. A plan could include a prearranged signal from the faculty member that allows a student to leave the classroom briefly to spend time in a low-stimulation environment or to engage discreetly in stimming, a behavior such as rocking or hand flapping that provides comfort to the student but may distract others. Other options include allowing students with ASD to choose their seats (and help make sure they remain available), to wear hats or sunglasses, or to use earplugs or noise-canceling headphones. Some students benefit from permission to keep a small stress or comfort item such as a fidget toy, as long as it does not disturb others (Wheeler, n.d.).

Anxiety/coping behaviors. Individuals with ASD frequently describe themselves as dealing with tremendous anxiety and stress. Although the anxiety may be general and pervasive in nature, it may also be triggered by sensory overstimulation, social and communication expectations, or transitions and unexpected changes. These stressors may result in behavior that can seem unusual or rude. Unfortunately for students with ASD, faculty and peers often do not realize that the behaviors are not intended to be disruptive but are used as coping or self-soothing strategies.

A prearranged escape plan and access to comfort objects are useful strategies, but sometimes students who are having coping difficulties might not realize when they are being disruptive and need to excuse themselves. As suggested for sensory overload, instructors and students can agree on cues that the instructor can use to signal to the student that it is time to take a break. Similarly, a signal can be prearranged for students to cue their instructors when they are feeling overwhelmed and in need of a break or other assistance.

Cognitive flexibility/learning approach. Students on the spectrum may show some significant cognitive deficits at the same time that they excel in many aspects of academic performance. They may become easily bored with repetitive tasks and impatient with peers who are slower at processing. Typically, difficulty in considering alternative perspectives impacts critical thinking (Shmulsky & Gobbo, 2013). Lack of self-awareness sometimes results in students not realizing they are in academic difficulty until it is too late to recover and earn passing grades.

Even when they exhibit extraordinary expertise in chosen areas of interest, some students may struggle with executive functions such as planning, organizing, meeting deadlines, and adapting to change and transitions (Parker & Boutelle, 2009). Strategies that support students with EF issues include providing interim deadlines or check-ins with professors to gauge progress and checklists for monitoring steps of long-range projects. It is often helpful to give students the option of drawing on an area of expertise when choosing readings or assignment topics because this enhances their motivation to engage with the topic. Students benefit when instructors clarify expectations for work products by offering models, demonstrations, and other examples that meet and do not meet standards. It may be possible to pair students with peer mentors who can provide feedback and an additional layer of accountability and offer structure that assists a student with ASD to stay on task with assignments. It is important to remind students, however, that peer mentors are not responsible for ensuring that a student completes work, much less ensuring that the mentee is successful.

Motor skills. Fine and gross motor skills, as well as motor planning skills, are often areas of challenge for students with ASD. Fine motor skills such as writing, drawing, turning pages, using utensils, playing instruments, using locks and keys, and manipulating small objects may be limited or impossible, depending on the severity of a student's condition. Furthermore, gross motor skill challenges may affect a student's ability to walk (e.g., they may have odd gait), run, sit, or balance.

Possible accommodations for motor skills difficulties include allowing students to use computers for in-class work, tests, and assignments; providing a note taker; providing models and step-by-step instructions; providing extra time for assignments, tests, and quizzes; and providing readers or scribes for in-class assignments or assessments. Further accommodations might be needed to provide access to students with ASD enrolled in courses that draw on fine or gross motor skills, such as physical education, visual arts, and lab courses (Wheeler, n.d.). Figure 4.3 summarizes strategies for creating a more welcoming classroom environment for students with ASD.

Supporting Students in Online Environments

Online and hybrid classes have rapidly become permanent fixtures of the postsecondary environment, bringing both challenges and benefits to students who learn differently. "Some places have let the drive to offer online instruction get ahead of thoughtful planning," says L. Scott Lissner (past president of AHEAD). "I think there are a number of institutions that do it well—whether it is offering captioning or print access or helping the quadriplegic student—but there are enough places that are not doing it well" (as cited in Haynie, 2014, ¶7). Given the newness of the field, it is not surprising that relatively little research has been conducted on how students with LD fare in online education, but initial findings show a range of issues that preferentially advantage some students with disabilities while posing problems for others. Online courses rely heavily on text-based communication formats, challenging students with language-based difficulties, and their asynchronous nature presents barriers to students who struggle with scheduling, attendance, and timely work completion (UDI Online Project, 2010).

Classroom Checklist
- Prepare the student for all changes in routine and/or environment.
- Use verbal cues, clear visual demonstrations, and physical cues.
- Avoid abstract ideas when possible. When abstract ideas are necessary, use visual cues as an aid.
- Understand that an increase in unusual or difficult behaviors probably indicates an increase in stress, in which case ask the student if he or she would like to talk with you.
- Do not take misbehavior personally.
- Avoid nicknames such as Pal, Buddy, Wise Guy; idioms (e.g., "save your breath," "jump the gun," "second thoughts"); double meanings, sarcasm, and teasing.
- Break tasks down into smaller steps or present them in more than one way (i.e., visually, verbally, and physically).
- Avoid verbal overload.
- Be aware that for some individuals, what might seem like ordinary classroom auditory and visual input can, in fact, represent perceptual extremes of too much or too little.
- Use writing if a student uses repetitive verbal arguments and/or questions, requesting she write down the argumentative statement or question, and then write your reply. Or try writing her argument and/or question yourself, and then ask the student to write a logical reply.

Figure 4.3. ASD-friendly classroom checklist. Adapted from "Reasonable Accommodations: A Faculty Guide to Teaching Students with Disabilities." http://www.ccny.cuny.edu/sites/default/files/2014-Reasonable-Accommodations-Faculty-Guide-to-Teaching-Students-with-Disabilities.pdf. Used with permission.

Text-Based Challenges

Although online courses may feature audio and video, students tend to communicate with each other and instructors primarily via chatroom-style digital discussions and by posting written responses to questions and assignments. This can be problematic for students with a language-based LD such as dyslexia, who may excel in classroom discussions and oral presentations while struggling with reading and writing text. Their online postings may include spelling and mechanical errors that color others' perceptions of their performance. Composing a written response can be excessively time-consuming and frustrating, especially compared to presenting an oral opinion during a face-to-face class. Most course content, including directions for assignments and instructions about due dates for quizzes, tests, and projects, are in a text-based format. Therefore, it is critical that instructors use learning management systems (e.g., Blackboard, Canvas, Moodle) and select text-based content (e.g., readings and directions) that is fully accessible to individuals who rely on TTS technology to hear it. This also allows students with a range of reading difficulties to personalize the reading experience by altering margins, fonts, text size, color, and background colors.

At the same time, students with ASD who have difficulty with social communication may not only excel with written discussion formats but also feel liberated from the anxiety that accompanies their relations with peers during class conversations and collaborations.

Their communication difficulties in online courses may stem from difficulty interpreting assignment expectations regarding length and depth, especially when the assignment involves considering an issue from multiple perspectives. Captioning videos, although designed to accommodate students with impaired hearing, may benefit students with ASD or ADHD, and even students without disabilities, by helping them focus on content while minimizing the confusions they experience from nonverbal elements of the presentation, such as body language, tone of voice, and, possibly, distracting background noise or music (Morris et al., 2016).

Executive Function Challenges

Students with ADHD and EF challenges appear to struggle with asynchronous online courses due to the very aspect that makes asynchronous courses appealing to many other students: their flexibility. As the authors of the UDI Online Project noted, online courses "require increased self-management and executive functioning skills" much more than their face-to-face counterparts (Madaus, McKeown, Gelbar, & Banerjee, 2012, p. 21).

Although students with ADHD, who tend to be night owls, may appreciate being able to participate in the wee hours of the night, the reality is that the absence of regularly scheduled meetings presents pitfalls for timely participation and work completion. Furthermore, the lack of personal, face-to-face relationships with faculty makes it harder for some students to feel the urgency of deadlines, and they experience a diminished sense of accountability that might otherwise be fostered when a student is part of a real-time learning community. The UDI Online Project's research team reported that both faculty and students cite the lack of face-to-face interactions and immediate feedback as impediments to learning (Madaus et al., 2012).

Best Practices for Online Environments

Many of the suggestions from research on supportive practices for students with LD in online classes will benefit all students. Crum (cited in Kelly, 2010) surveyed disability service offices about the ways online instructors can help students succeed and found that proactive, frequent communication; early and compassionate response to low participation or inadequate completion of assignments; and one-on-one support when a student shows signs of struggle, followed by suggestions that a student access additional help from an advisor or online tutoring center were among the most frequently recommended strategies. They also recommend providing detailed feedback on submitted assignments in order to foster a personal connection with the instructor, which is harder to achieve in virtual settings than in face-to-face classes. A personalized dialogue with the instructor increases the likelihood a student will actively seek guidance when confused or frustrated (UDI Online Project, 2010).

Other recommended practices specifically target students who learn differently. Researchers at the University of Connecticut developed a collection of instructional strategies and digital tools for instructors of online courses (see Figure 4.4) as part of their Department of Education-funded Universal Design for Instruction Online Project.

Evaluating Digital Tools
- **Accessibility:** Can the tool be obtained easily (either downloaded from the Internet or purchased through a campus store)?
- **Usability:** Is the tool easy to learn and use by both faculty and students?
- **Effectiveness:** Can the tool meet a need identified by faculty and/or students during the needs assessment?
- **Cost:** Is the tool free or low-cost, and could an individual instructor purchase the tool using available department funds?
- **Application of UDI:** Does the tool assist faculty in applying the construct of UDI?

Figure 4.4. Criteria for evaluation of digital tools (University of Connecticut, UDI Online Project, 2010).

Once evaluated, the tools were organized according to the type of access they provide: cognitive, communication, or physical. They vary considerably and include free, stand-alone resources easily accessed from the Internet such as Google Chat, Survey Monkey, Skype, and Doodle as well as those that require a software purchase or license, such as Camtasia and Adobe Pro. Although the eToolbox (available online at www.udi.uconn. edu) has not been updated since the project was completed in 2012, it remains a useful compendium of information for faculty when designing and delivering online instruction. The researchers caution that eTools are constantly evolving; therefore, faculty should also seek updated versions of these tools, as well as entirely new ones. Other websites that review tech tools include the following:

- Ed Tech Reviews (http://edtechreview.in/reviews),
- *International Journal for Educational Technology* (https://educationaltechnology.net/ijet/index.php/ijet),
- *JSET – Journal of Special Education Technology* (journals.sagepub.com/home/jst), and
- TechMatrix (http://techmatrix.org).

Universal Design

Although the UD movement originated as a set of design principles for architects and engineers responding to the requirements of the Americans with Disabilities Act for more accessible and usable environments, this framework for disability rights made a quick jump into educational communities. McGuire, Scott, and Shaw (2006) published some of the earliest work that adapted the principles of UD to benefit students in the learning environment. In the same way that replacing a set of stairs with a ramp benefits not just wheelchair users but also users of baby strollers, rolling suitcases, delivery carts, and crutches, universally designed instructional approaches can proactively meet the needs of a broad range of learners. The UD concept for education developed as "an approach to teaching that consists of the proactive design and use of inclusive instructional strategies that benefit a broad range of learners, including students with disabilities" (McGuire et al. 2006, p. 169). One of its key tenets is that it normalizes cognitive diversity/heterogeneity without lowering academic standards.

Following UD principles, educators can provide students with cognitive ramps (i.e., approaches that are built into the curriculum from the beginning, rather than added retroactively as individual accommodations) to enhance learning for diverse cognitive profiles. UD does not promise to eliminate individualized accommodations, but it reduces the need for them by offering options that minimize many of the barriers faced by individuals with disabilities. One example of a broadly beneficial cognitive ramp is a statement in the syllabus that expresses the value of learner diversity within the classroom community as it enriches the classroom culture with a range of perspectives and approaches to learning. It is helpful to discuss that statement during the opening days of the semester. This can be followed by inviting students to discuss individual learning needs privately with the instructor during regular office hours or before or after class.

Another concrete example of a widely beneficial UD practice is ensuring accessibility of all course content. This includes providing texts and readings in digital formats that can be read by a variety of screen readers across many devices, including smartphones and tablets; closed captioning on all videos; and alt-text for visuals.

Of particular importance to postsecondary institutions is that UD be implemented without altering essential educational requirements or watering down the curriculum. Universal design is often formalized as a set of principles that encourage faculty to apply design principles that are consonant with their disciplinary traditions and their personal approach to teaching. Universal design for instruction (UDI), developed at the University of Connecticut, adapts the seven original principles of universal design for the built environment and adds two that are specific to the classroom (see Figure 4.5; Scott, Shaw, & McGuire, in press).

The Center for Applied and Specialized Technology has also developed robust resources at the National Center on Universal Design for Learning, using a different model of UD principles they call universal design for learning (UDL). The UDL model is based on three primary neural networks in the brain activated by learning: the affective, recognition, and strategic networks. The model includes three related principles of UDL: (a) multiple means of engagement, (b) multiple means of presentation, and (c) multiple means of expression.

These form a pedagogic framework for designing and delivering instruction, primarily by offering options for learners to adapt or modify the user experience according to their needs and preferences.

UDI Principles
1. Equitable use: accessible by all. Provide identical when possible, equivalent when not
2. Flexible use: provide choice in methods of use
3. Simple and intuitive: instruction is straightforward and predictable; reduce complexity
4. Perceptible information: instruction is accessible regardless of student sensory abilities or ambient situation
5. Tolerance for error: anticipate variation in student learning pace and background
6. Low physical effort: minimize non-essential physical effort
7. Size and space for approach and use: students can participate regardless of body size, posture, mobility, or communication needs
8. Community of learners: promote interaction and communication among students as well as between students and instructor
9. Instructional climate: instruction is welcoming and inclusive, with high expectations for all

---

Figure 4.5. Universal design for instruction (UDI) principles from the University of Connecticut.

It is beyond the scope of this book to offer detailed directions for implementing UD, as it is not a prescriptive recipe but a philosophy and framework. Moreover, principles of UD should be applied in ways that align with essential course expectations across disciplines. However, for initial guidance, faculty can review the recommendations of the University of Washington's DO-IT Center (Disabilities, Opportunities, Internetworking, and Technology), outlined in Figure 4.6. Chapter 6 includes resources that offer specific examples and ongoing information that support educators in implementing the UD philosophy.

Conclusion

There are many ways for postsecondary educators to promote academic success for students with LD. Implementing accommodations mandated by the office of student disability services is a minimal first step that is required by law but also helps level the playing field by reducing the impact of unintentional barriers. Understanding the strengths as well as characteristic difficulties experienced by students with specific cognitive profiles helps educators minimize those barriers as they design and deliver instruction. Finally, implementing a UD approach promotes an academic culture that embraces cognitive heterogeneity for its positive contributions to the classroom experience while broadening access to the widest range of learners.

Recommendations for Universal Design

- Include a statement in your syllabus inviting students to talk with you and the disability services office about disability-related issues.
- Point out campus resources available to all students, such as tutoring centers, study skills labs, counseling centers, and computer labs.
- Clearly and early in a course define course requirements, announce the dates of exams, and tell students when assignments are due. Avoid last-minute readings or additional assignments and provide advance notice of changes in assignments and due dates.
- Provide printed materials early to allow students sufficient time to read and comprehend the material. Many students with learning disabilities find it beneficial to use software that can read the textbook and other text-based materials aloud. In order for them to take advantage of this technology, the printed text must first be converted into an electronic file. This process can be time-consuming.
- Use multi-modal methods to present classroom material, in order to address a variety of learning styles and strengths (e.g., auditory, visual, kinesthetic). Provide important information in both oral and written formats.
- When teaching a lesson, state objectives, review previous lessons, and summarize periodically.
- Use more than one way to demonstrate or explain information.
- Read aloud what you write on the board or present on an overhead visual.
- Keep instructions brief and uncomplicated. Repeat them word-for-word.
- Allow time for clarification of directions and essential information.
- Use captioned videos and know how to turn on the captioning feature. Although captioned videos are typically used for students who are deaf, they also help some students with learning disabilities and those for whom English is a second language, by ensuring content is presented visually and audibly. Give all students an opportunity to view a video multiple times (e.g., by making it available in a library or learning center, or on a website).
- Provide study guides or review sheets.
- Have multiple methods for course assessment, such as allowing students to take an exam or writing a paper; work alone or in a group; or deliver an oral, written, or videotaped project presentation.
- Stress organization and ideas rather than mechanics when grading in-class writing assignments and assessments.
- Design distance learning courses with accessibility in mind. For example, avoid real-time chat sessions, because not all students can type quickly or accurately enough to participate fully.

Figure 4.6 UD recommendations from University of Washington's DO-IT Center.

Chapter 5

Outside the Classroom: Cocurricular Issues for Students With LD

The cocurriculum can be thought of as the out-of-class experiences that enrich, extend, and complement the academic curriculum (Dalton & Crosby, 2012). These activities should be connected to the institutional mission, intentional, and rigorous; they include, but are not limited to, student research experiences, diversity workshops, service-learning opportunities, and sponsored speakers (Dalton & Crosby, 2012). Considerations for involving students in cocurricular experiences, especially high-impact activities, are discussed in Chapter 4.

Unlike opportunities that are part of the cocurriculum, extracurricular activities are not formally connected to the curriculum. For example, a Spanish major's participation in the video game club would likely be considered an extracurricular activity, whereas engagement in a Latinx heritage month speaker series sponsored by the Spanish department would be an example of a cocurricular activity. Despite their different emphases, both cocurricular and extracurricular activities can be beneficial to students (Kim & Bastedo, 2016; Webber, Krylow, & Zhang, 2013). As such, for the purposes of this chapter, cocurricular and extracurricular activities will be referred to simply as activities.

Only some of the learning that takes place outside the classroom occurs through formal experiences (e.g., programs and services) offered by college faculty and administrators. Much of the learning happening outside the classroom is informal, facilitated through daily interactions students have with peers in their residence hall rooms, at a dining hall table, or walking to class, among other things. Often, the learning gained through these informal experiences is just as meaningful, rich, and important as the learning that takes place through more formal, structured activities. However, administrators and faculty members have less direct influence over these informal learning experiences.

Such experiences, often associated with student affairs, academic advising, and academic support offices, can be beneficial to the success of students with disabilities, including those with LD (Newman et al., in press). To date, very little has been published on the out-of-class engagement of students with LD (Lalor, 2017; Lombardi & Lalor, 2017; Peña, 2014). Given that the amount of time spent outside the classroom constitutes the vast majority of a college student's week, the lack of research is both perplexing and concerning. We attempt to fill this void by discussing how out-of-class experiences can facilitate or hinder success for students with LD. A particular focus of attention is the ways in which faculty, administrators, and staff can support the transition of students with LD in five broad areas within student and academic life: (a) academic support services and advising, (b) health and wellness, (c) residence life, (d) student engagement in out-of-class activities, and (e) student conduct.

Academic Support Services and Advising

Although connected to the curriculum, academic advising and academic support services are typically engaged outside of class time. As such, for the purposes of this book, they are considered out-of-class activities. For students with disabilities, use of academic advising and academic support services can be important for persistence in higher education (DuPaul, Dahlstrom-Hakki, et al., 2017; Newman et al., in press; Troiano, Liefeld, & Trachtenberg, 2010). Academic support services vary from institution to institution; however, common components include academic advising, writing services/support, quantitative services/support, testing services, and tutoring.

> **"** One of the barriers I see is incoming students just not knowing help is there. Students don't always notice that little disability statement in every syllabus, and faculty don't always emphasize it (they have a lot to cover!). Also, some students just don't know that "disability" includes ADHD and ASD, so they aren't aware that our services are available to them. — *Lori Smith, EdD, Accommodations Coordinator, Student Disability Services, University of Tennessee* **"**

Academic Support

Given the nature of their difficulties, students with LD may seek out or may be encouraged to use academic support services (DuPaul, Dahlstrom-Hakki et al., 2017). Conversely, students with these disabilities may choose not to seek services from learning/academic specialists and tutors for many of the same reasons that they choose not to seek disability services, including (a) stigma, (b) desire to try college without special academic supports, and (c) lack of awareness of their availability (Marshak, Van Wieren, Ferrell, Swiss, & Dugan, 2010). All students should be allowed to make their own decisions regarding their use of academic support services, but all students should be aware of their existence and availability. Faculty, staff, and administrators who work in these centers should know how to work with students with disabilities at various entry points (e.g., at the beginning of a course, when the student feels as though they are falling behind, after a student experiences failure).

Using the principles of universal design in developing academic support services can ensure adequate supports for students with LD, even if they choose not to identify as such. Higbee and Eaton (2008) offered a variety of suggestions for employing UD principles of in learning centers, including

- providing all materials (e.g., descriptions of services, handouts) in multiple formats (e.g., large font, electronic format);

- developing policies (e.g., no cell phone areas, quiet areas) and physical spaces (e.g., sound-absorbing materials, partitions between study spaces) that reduce noise levels; and

- allowing time for "translation" and "processing" when delivering instruction and tutoring.

Academic Advising

Academic advising is ubiquitous on college campuses. As such, advisors can, and often do, play a pivotal role in the college student experience. Most advisors will at some point in their careers work with a student with LD (Preece et al., 2007). In fact, the advisor may be the first person to whom a student discloses their disability given concerns about stigma and disability-related discrimination (Hartman-Hall & Haaga, 2002). With this in mind, it is essential for advisors to understand that the disability is but a single facet of the student and should not dictate their academic or cocurricular path.

Advisors can play an important role in helping students obtain accommodations or support services from their institution's disability services office. As such, advisors should know how and when to refer a student with LD to disability services (Preece et al., 2007). When students express or suggest that they are or anticipate facing barriers to academic or student life, a referral should be made to disability services. Similarly, if a student expresses or suggests that they have been the target of discrimination related to their disability, referrals should be made to an ADA coordinator, campus police, the student conduct office, or another party outlined in the institution's anti-discrimination policy. There are times when referrals to disability services or another disability-related office (e.g., counseling, health services, ADA coordinator) are warranted and appropriate; however, students with disabilities should not be referred to these offices any time they have an issue. For example, a referral of a student with dyslexia to disability services because they are struggling with a romantic relationship would be inappropriate, as this is not an access issue. In that case, a referral to a counselor may be more appropriate. A student with a learning disability, ADHD, and/or ASD does not *belong* to disability services and should have access to the same services and supports as their neurotypical peers.

Other critical roles of advisors include helping students plan accessible academic programs and ensuring that approved accommodations associated with course selection are enacted. The advisor and advisee should carefully review a student's plan of study to make sure that it aligns with their aspirations and interests. During this process, potential curricular challenges may be identified so that they can be met proactively. Some advisees with LD may express the need for a course substitution or waiver. For example, a foreign language substitution or waiver for a student with a language-based learning disability may be appropriate. Policies on course substitutions and waivers vary from institution to institution but are generally not available if the substitution or waiver lowers academic standards or constitutes a substantial alteration to the program of study. Advisors are encouraged to learn about their institution's policies on course waivers and substitutions.

A reduced course load is another accommodation that students with LD may consider. For some students, a standard full-time course load may not be possible. For example, a student may take longer to read course material, write papers, interpret questions, process numbers, organize assignments, or study for and take exams. Given the extra time and energy it takes for students with these difficulties, enrolling in fewer courses may be a necessary and reasonable accommodation. Academic advisors may need to work with students to request this accommodation and, if received, help to plan an academic program that takes the reduced course load into consideration.

Although an advisee may disclose a disability to their advisor, this is not always the case. As noted by Dyer (2008), academic advisors should always ask questions that develop advisor–advisee rapport and allow the advisor to understand the needs of the advisee. Questions such as "What specific needs do you have?" or "How can we work together to ensure that the advising process is effective for you?" serve as starting points for this dialogue (Dyer, 2008, ¶9). It is important for advisors to know that although a diagnosis is necessary for obtaining disability-related accommodations, most students with LD will not formally disclose their disability to their institution. In fact, some college students may never have struggled academically prior to being faced by the increased rigor of college academics, and they may be unaware that they have a learning difference. Actively listening to what students say and asking follow-up questions may provide keen insight into which academic support services could benefit them.

In addition to course selection and degree planning, academic advisors are uniquely positioned to assist students with identifying and considering cocurricular experiences that will complement their academic programs and personal goals. For example, internships, workshops on diversity, service-learning activities, learning communities, and research opportunities are all experiences that have been linked to increased retention and graduation rates (Kuh, 2008) and that connect to student educational goals.

Advisors can help facilitate connections to the cocurriculum and support students with disabilities as they plan to engage in such activities. As noted in Chapter 2, some students with LD experience challenges associated with EF. As such, planning how and when to engage in activities can be difficult. Advisors who are aware that a student has difficulty with planning and managing a schedule, staying on task, and making decisions might consider helping a student plan their activities using a calendar or another organizational system. If an advisor is lacking the time or skills associated with developing organizational systems, they can provide a referral to another resource on campus that might be able to support the student with such a task. Some students have high anxiety that can result in limited engagement. An advisor who knows that a student has social anxiety may be able to assist by discussing strategies for meeting new people, helping the student identify supports they can take advantage of (e.g., attending with a friend), and thinking through the benefits that can be accrued by participating. Conversely, although the benefits of engagement in the cocurriculum are clear, some students may be overengaged in activities at the expense of academic preparation, sleep, and other health-related behaviors. Given the nature of the advisor–advisee relationship, advisors may be able to help students to identify when they are overcommitted and to develop strategies for resetting priorities.

Health and Wellness

Maintaining health and wellness is critical for all college students, and many of them will struggle with achieving healthy lifestyles while in college. Students with LD are no different, though they may present some unique challenges for campus staff. Professional and paraprofessional staff in health services, counseling services, health education, residence life, dining services, athletics, and the office of the dean of students are among those on the front lines for supporting health and wellness initiatives and should be well informed about the challenges faced by students with LD as they transition to higher education.

Medication Management

Some, but certainly not all, students with LD come to college with prescription medications. Students with ADHD may arrive with any number of medications, including Adderall, Concerta, Ritalin, and Strattera, among others. Students with ASD and learning disabilities also may have been prescribed medications to manage behaviors (e.g., hyperactivity and aggression) and to treat co-occurring psychiatric disabilities (e.g., generalized anxiety disorder and major depressive disorder). For some students, college may be the first time they are managing their own medications, as parents or other caretakers may have largely coordinated this in high school (Meaux, Green, & Broussard, 2009). Scheduling appointments with doctors, ensuring that medications are taken on schedule, refilling prescriptions, managing copays, and understanding drug interaction effects may be new expectations of students transitioning to college. Given these new responsibilities, it is not surprising that a substantial number of students fail to adhere to medication protocols provided by doctors and pharmacists (Meaux et al., 2009).

Students should know what medications they are taking, the correct dosage, and the frequency of doses. Health services professionals and counselors are encouraged to discuss medications directly with students in order to help them implement strategies for taking medications as directed and managing their own health care. For example, students can be encouraged to make use of natural supports (e.g., cell phones and computers) to keep track of medications taken and correct dosages and to set reminders to take medications on time. Health services professionals might also recommend keeping medications next to an alarm clock that students set each evening and turn off each morning or placing a reminder note on the room door.

Most faculty, staff, and administrators will never need to know which medications students are taking. However, it is important for all members of the campus community to be aware that students may falter when taking medications. Some students may decide that they no longer want or need to take medication without consulting medical or counseling professionals (Meaux et al., 2009). Failure to take medications as prescribed or simply stopping their use can have adverse effects, including insomnia, severe headaches, dizziness, depression, fatigue, irregular heartbeat, irritability, and nausea. Although this may go without saying, when such symptoms are observed or if a student notes experiencing such symptoms, faculty and staff should encourage the student to seek medical care. If particularly severe symptoms are observed, such as suicidal ideation, emergency personnel should be contacted immediately.

Relationships and Sexuality

Like many young adults, the transition to college offers students with LD greater freedom. No longer having parents and caretakers looking over their shoulder, students have opportunities to express themselves more freely and to explore their sexuality. However, students with LD sometimes lack extensive knowledge regarding sexual health. One reason is that some students were removed from health education courses in K-12 education to receive additional academic services. Another explanation for why students may lack knowledge is that some K-12 educators and parents view students with disabilities as nonsexual beings (Barnett & Maticka-Tyndale, 2015; Sullivan & Caterino, 2008). As a result, the possibility of sexual relationships in college can lead to great excitement as well as anxiety for some students.

Developing a sense of sexual identity, pursuing relationships, and engaging in sexual activity may also be complicated when a student identifies as a person with a disability or shows manifestations of the disability. For students with ASD, for example, pursuing romantic relationships can be complicated by challenges associated with communication. As discussed in Chapter 2, students with ASD often communicate in ways that are noticeably different from their peers. For example, a student with difficulty in expressive communication may repeat a question multiple times and may be seen as inattentive, rude, or intentionally harassing. Students with ASD may also have differences in receptive language or have difficulty interpreting nonverbal forms of communication or recognizing figurative language.

Given the high degree of interpersonal communication involved in romantic relationships, difficulties may arise for students with ASD.

Students with LD who identify as LGBTQ may experience additional challenges because they have multiple marginalized identities. According to Henry, Fuerth, and Figliozzi (2010) and colleagues, disability and sexual orientation are compartmentalized and rarely considered together. Essentially, explorations of disability tend to be examined from a heterosexual lens, and sexual orientation tends to be examined from a nondisabled lens. As such, services offered by counseling, disability services, and health services tend to ignore larger issues of intersectionality and compound experiences of marginalization. Because the research literature offers limited guidance on this topic, students with intersecting identities may be further marginalized (Croteau & Talbot, 2000). Faculty, staff, and administrators are encouraged to be cognizant of how and when LBGTQ identity intersects with a student's identity as an individual with a learning difference.

Eating, Sleeping, and Hygiene

Some students with LD experience issues related to eating, sleeping, and hygiene. As has been discussed, with the transition to college comes greater independence and responsibility for students. It is not uncommon for students, with or without disabilities, to have difficulty adjusting to the new demands of college life.

Most students have been told at one point or another that eating a balanced diet, exercising regularly, getting a good night's sleep, and maintaining proper hygiene are important to being healthy. So why do so many students struggle with eating, sleeping, and hygiene? For some students with LD, particularly those with ADHD, the problem is frequently related to difficulties with EF. As discussed in Chapter 2, EF encompasses the cognitive abilities involved in planning, remembering, initiating, or delaying an activity. It also regulates an individual's ability to sustain self-directed behavior toward a goal. Among the aspects of EF with which students may struggle are initiation or activation, focus, effort, and action (see Chapter 4). Going to sleep on time, eating nutritious meals, and maintaining "proper" hygiene all require that students employ EF skills. When faced with stressors (e.g., increased and more challenging academic workloads, new social situations), executive functioning is reduced (Starcke, Wiesen, Trotzke, & Brand, 2016), meaning students have less bandwidth to maintain basic health behaviors even when they understand the importance of those behaviors. In the past, parents or other caretakers may have stepped in to fill the gap created by reduced EF, but students will need to develop new support structures to manage those challenges in college.

For students with ASD, problems in self-care may be related to EF, but they may also stem from not knowing the social norms surrounding personal care, being unaware of the social implications of violating those norms, or simply deciding not to adhere to established norms. For example, although some students with ASD ignore hygiene care because they do not recognize its social value, other students may avoid it because heightened sensitivity to stimuli may make daily routines of bathing and brushing teeth physically uncomfortable. Similarly, some students with ASD fail to maintain a healthy diet because of strong aversions to specific tastes and rigidly maintaining prescribed diets, not because they lack knowledge or awareness of what constitutes a well-balanced diet.

Faculty, staff, and administrators can support students with ASD in understanding social norms. Concrete language that is direct yet respectful can be particularly helpful for many students. Students may be well aware of the implications of failing to eat, sleep, and maintain proper hygiene but may avoid these activities if they are unaware of the social rules governing related behaviors. For example, students may avoid going to the dining hall if they are unsure how much space to leave between themselves and the person next to them in the serving line or how to choose a place to sit.

Alcohol and Other Drug Use

The use of alcohol and other drugs (AOD) on college campuses continues to receive great attention. A 2016 national study of AOD use among young adults showed that illicit drug use was lower among college students than their peers not enrolled in college (Schulenberg, Johnston, O'Malley, Bachman, Miech, & Patrick, 2017). However, college students engaged in heavy drinking and got drunk more often than their non-college peers. West, Graham, and Temple (2017) further noted that students with disabilities who had recently used drugs (other than alcohol) were more likely to binge drink than their peers who had not used drugs (other than alcohol). In particular, students who used marijuana or amphetamines were significantly more likely to binge drink than students with disabilities who did not use these drugs. This finding is of particular importance to students with LD because Adderall is an amphetamine frequently prescribed to students with ADHD.

Addiction to AOD has long been considered highly comorbid (i.e., co-occurring) with ADHD (Kessler et al., 2006). Although an explanation for the high co-occurrence of ADHD and substance abuse is still emerging, it is clear that students with ADHD are prone to experimenting with alcohol, illegal drugs, and tobacco at an earlier age than their peers (Molina et al., 2007). College and university faculty, staff, and administrators should be aware of this high co-occurrence and proactively develop programming and support services to meet the needs of this student population. As with other areas of campus life, materials and programs to address AOD that are designed according to UD philosophy are likely to be effective for students with LD. Mental health and counseling staff should be trained to work with students with LD on the topic of AOD.

Living on Campus

For nearly three decades, research has suggested that living on a college campus is linked to positive learning and psychosocial outcomes for students (Pascarella & Terenzini, 1991). According to Ballou, Reavill, and Schultz (1995), students living on campus experience a variety of benefits associated with social engagement and interactions with institutional faculty, staff, and administrators. Living in residence halls is predictive of increased retention and graduation rates (Oseguera & Rhee, 2009; Schudde, 2011), and students with disabilities who live on campus are more likely to persist than students with disabilities who do not live on campus (Mamiseishvili & Koch, 2011). Pascarella and Terenzini (1991) note that "those residence climates with the strongest impacts on cognitive development and persistence are typically the result of purposeful programmatic efforts to integrate the student's intellectual and social life during college" (p. 613).

At the same time, living away from home is a new experience for many students, complete with new expectations for student conduct and behavior. Although most students will be sharing a room with one or more roommates, all students will be sharing common spaces such as lounges, bathrooms, and hallways. Indeed, the transition to living on a college campus is complex and fraught with new experiences and situations that must be navigated by all students, and the particular difficulties that students with LD may face when living on campus are worthy of added consideration.

66

Making the transition from high school to college is tough and making the switch from having a well-known daily schedule and consistent daily external accountability checkers (e.g., parents, teachers, siblings, friends, boyfriend/girlfriend) takes time to adjust to. Who will you study with? Who will you touch base with to make sure you're doing your work, on track to meet deadlines, who will you get your emotional support from? These things take time to figure out at college, while putting together a new routine for classes, homework, chores, social and campus activities, and making your own appointments. — *Alicia Brandon, Assistant Director, Student Accessibility Services, Dartmouth College* 99

Intentional residential programming that meets the broad needs of all students as well as the more specific needs of diverse student populations can help students navigate these new challenges and expectations. Residence hall administrators are encouraged to incorporate a discussion of UD principles into training for professional and student staff and to model the UD philosophy in the design and delivery of the training. For example, program and training materials should be provided in multiple accessible formats (e.g., printed text, electronic format, Braille), content should be delivered using common language (e.g., limited acronyms and jargon), and learning outcomes should be assessed using multiple methods (e.g., conversations, quizzes, authentic assessments). Additionally, the challenges faced by students with LD are often similar to those faced by other students whether or not they have a disability. Programs that address such topics as health and wellness, study skills and strategies, independent living, executive functioning, and socialization on a college campus can benefit many students living in residence halls.

A common aspect of the residential experience is living in a small community. Although housing configurations vary greatly within and between institutions (e.g., single or double room, suites, apartments, living–learning communities, theme floors or houses), most students will find themselves in situations where they have to interact with other residents. Alpern and Zager (2007) noted, "adolescent conversations are rapid, abstract, filled with figurative and nonliteral references, and dependent on the ability to take another's perspective" (p. 428). As noted in Chapter 2, students with ASD frequently have difficulty with figurative language (e.g., idiom, sarcasm, metaphor), which they sometimes interpret literally, resulting in miscommunication. When a request for "a few minutes of alone time" is met by a student with ASD barging in three minutes later, tempers may flare (particularly if the roommate making the request was in the midst of having a romantic moment with a partner). Given their difficulties with receptive and expressive communication, it is not surprising that a recent study reported that only 43% of students with ASD found it easy to get along with their college roommates (Gelbar, Shefcyk, & Reichow, 2015).

Roommate situations can also be challenging for students who are looking for quiet environments in which to complete work or to relax. By design, residence halls are often lively and stimulating environments. For students who are highly distractible, sensitive to stimuli (e.g., noise, smells), or in need of long periods of time to complete work, the residence hall environment can be a challenge. Although housing accommodations (e.g., single rooms, quiet housing) are available at most institutions, they are provided on a case-by-case basis. For students with ASD, receiving a single room is a fairly common accommodation (Brown, 2017; Gelbar et al., 2015), but the impact is mixed. Some students find the decrease in extraneous stimulation associated with the single room to be helpful, whereas others say the single room increases isolation (Gelbar et al., 2015; Sarkis, 2008).

Again, although a single occupancy room may be an appropriate accommodation for some students, disability service providers should be aware of the additional housing options that often exist. For example, lower occupancy rooms (e.g., a double), suite/pod style rooms, and rooms in a designated "quiet" residence hall may meet student needs for reduced distractions while facilitating the transition to social life on campus (Sarkis, 2008). Residence hall staff are encouraged to discuss the wide variety of housing options available on their campus with disability service staff, because a disability services professional will be determining the accommodation. Together, the disability services office and the residential life staff can collaborate to ensure that students with LD have their needs met in a way that affords greatest access to all that residential living has to offer.

A final residential issue that can be challenging for students with LD is living with others in an environment with community expectations (i.e., rules). As discussed in Chapter 2, students with ASD are often inflexible in their thinking. When it comes to established rules and community expectations, students may view behaviors as either correct (i.e., adhering to the rules) or incorrect (i.e., violating the rules). For example, students with ASD living in residence halls designated as quiet housing may be challenged by the term quiet, which is subjective. Working with students on the spectrum to determine what a quiet environment looks and sounds like may be necessary. For example, residence hall staff may benefit from explicitly discussing with students the difference between quiet and silent. Unfortunately, students on the spectrum are frequently left to navigate these less-than-clear policies and rules without support, resulting in conflicts with roommates, peers, and residence hall staff.

Engagement in Out-of-Class Activities

The out-of-class learning opportunities afforded to today's college students are diverse and plentiful. Like their neurotypical peers, students with diverse cognitive profiles are engaged in all facets of campus life. Because of the invisible nature of LD, however, faculty and administrators are frequently unaware that students with diverse cognitive profiles are participating. Sometimes faculty and administrators will be provided with letters indicating that students are entitled to accommodations, but research suggests that only 35% of postsecondary students with disabilities even disclose their disability to their institution's disability services office (Newman & Madaus, 2015b). As such, the likelihood of knowing that a student has a learning disability, ADHD, or ASD is quite small.

Minimal literature describes the activities in which the general population of students with disabilities engage, much less students with LD. The literature that does exist suggests that students with disabilities engage in many of the same activities as their peers without disabilities, such as athletics, leadership and activist activities, and residence life (Stout & Schwartz, 2014; Wilus, 2013). Data from the National Survey of Student Engagement (NSSE) show that students with disabilities rate their campus environments as less supportive than their peers without disabilities do, even though they engage in similar activities (Hedrick, Dizén, Collins, Evans, & Grayson, 2010). The remainder of this section focuses on strategies for making traditional campus activities and leadership opportunities accessible to students representing a wide range of cognitive functioning.

Campus Activities and Events

Student involvement can be considered "the amount of physical and psychological energy that the student devotes to the academic experience" (Astin, 1999, p. 518). Examples of involvement offered by Astin (1999) include, but are not limited to, devoting considerable energy to studying; spending extensive amounts of time on campus; actively participating in student organizations; and interacting frequently with faculty, staff, and students. Though a number of benefits of student involvement have been identified, increased student retention and persistence have garnered much attention. Given the important benefits, additional efforts must be made to engage students with disabilities to ensure that students with LD are afforded opportunities to be involved in activities and events.

Institutions of higher education regularly sponsor events and activities for students, faculty, staff, and administrators alike. These events range from graduation ceremonies and lectures to concerts and parties to clubs and athletics and may be coordinated by any number of academic or administrative departments. As such, ensuring that events are accessible to all students is the responsibility of the entire campus community. Students with LD have the same right to access and engage in student life as their peers without LD. This right is afforded by both the ADA and Section 504 of the Rehabilitation Act. Although this book and this section are focused on learning disabilities, ADHD, and ASD in particular, event planners should make certain that all activities are accessible to all individuals with disabilities.

Universal design can be used to think through various aspects of a program (e.g., planning, evaluation, policy formation, venue selection, staffing, and technology) to address barriers before they impede access. Among the barriers students with learning disabilities often face are advertising presented solely in text format and the lack of available technology to facilitate reading at events that are based heavily on text. Barriers to full participation for students with ADHD include long programs without breaks held in spaces that offer an abundance of distracting stimuli. Students with ASD may also face barriers, such as loud music, strong odors, and bright lights that may be overwhelming or even painful to some students on the spectrum. Adopting UD principles will assist organizers in making all events and activities accessible to the widest number of people possible. Event planners are encouraged to visit the website for the DO-IT Center at the University of Washington (https://www.washington.edu/doit/about/overview) for resources and tools related to planning and organizing accessible events on college campuses.

Athletics, Club Sports, and Intramurals

Exercise is important for maintaining a healthy lifestyle. Among the benefits accrued by individuals who engage in regular physical exercise are improved cardiorespiratory fitness, strong bones and muscles, reduced symptoms of anxiety and depression, and a reduced likelihood of heart disease, cancer, and diabetes (Centers for Disease Control and Prevention, 2017). The U.S. Government Accountability Office (2010) emphasized the health and social benefits accrued by students with disabilities who engage in physical activity, noting that "[t]hese benefits may be even more important for children with disabilities [than their peers without disabilities]" (p. 1).

Although the ADA and Rehabilitation Act afforded students with disabilities equal opportunities for accessing athletics, club sports, and intramurals for which they were otherwise qualified, Van Rheenen, Grigorieff, and Adams (2017) noted that "few educational institutions, particularly within higher education, have met this national need" (p. 92). Although most barriers to athletic participation have focused on students who have orthopedic impairments, are blind, or are deaf, students with LD may also require additional consideration.

Participation in intercollegiate athletics, club sports, and intramurals often requires students to listen, memorize, plan, and communicate with others. Students with LD may find some of these activities difficult. Wilus (2013) offered a variety of suggestions for how athletic coaches can better support athletes with ADHD by adapting strategies for the classroom to the playing field. Among the strategies recommended by Wilus are (a) developing and posting a daily practice plan/schedule; (b) setting clear expectations and consequences for behavior; (c) delivering instruction on drills or plays in short, manageable chunks; (d) providing immediate feedback emphasizing the positive prior to the negative; (e) making the information interesting and applicable; and (f) presenting information in ways that use different modalities (e.g., written, verbal, interactive). The strategies offered by Wilus align with UD principles and can benefit a wide variety of learners.

All student athletes must balance academics and athletics. The schedule imposed by athletics may help students with LD maintain regular study and homework routines (particularly if study halls, tutoring, and other services are offered via athletics). Other students may find that the one-size-fits-all structure does not address their needs adequately. Coaches, advisors, and other support staff are encouraged to talk with each student about their learning needs and to collaborate with other campus departments to ensure that student athletes receive the services they need to succeed academically and athletically (Clark & Parette, 2002).

Participation in club sports and intramurals may also pose challenges for students with LD, particularly for students who assume leadership and coordination roles. Although frequently omitted from the literature of student leadership (Hall, Scott, & Borsz, 2008), the roles that students play in these organizations are extensive. Hall and colleagues noted that student leadership roles range from serving on governance boards and as club sport officers to serving as referees and field managers. In each of these leadership positions, students must use EF skills, maintain sustained attention, interact and communicate effectively with other students, and, in some cases, use reading and math skills (e.g., understanding policies, reading schedules, managing budgets, scorekeeping). Clearly, such expectations may be a challenge to meet for some students. Professionals working with club sports are encouraged to discuss with each student (regardless of whether they have LD) the strengths and areas of challenge they bring to the position. In cases where students disclose that they have LD that may make an aspect of the leadership role challenging, professionals should inquire about accommodations or supports that will allow for full and equitable engagement in the leadership experience. In many cases, this can be done without going through the formal accommodations process with disability services, but in some situations the student may need to be referred to disability services. For example, the provision of extra time to complete leadership tasks may not require an accommodation, but requests for speech-to-text technology in the club sports office may need to go through disability services to justify expenditures. Of particular importance is that professionals know that they can always contact disability services for guidance and recommendations as to how best to work with and serve students with LD.

Student Leadership

Many out-of-class activities can build leadership skills, such as participation in student government and serving as a resident assistant or orientation leader (Sessa, Alonso, Farago, Schettino, Tacchi, & Bragger, 2017). Leadership development is related to increased self-efficacy, engagement, character development, and personal development (Komives, Owen, Longerbeam, Mainella, & Osteen, 2005; Sessa et al., 2017). The development and fine-tuning of leadership skills are just as valuable for students with LD as they are for neurotypical students. Because students with disabilities must learn to speak up for themselves in order to receive accommodations in postsecondary environments, some could argue that leadership skills are particularly important for students with LD. In fact, leadership skills are essential components of self-advocacy (Wehmeyer, 1992).

Despite the importance of these skills, the literature on leadership education as it relates to students with disabilities tends to focus more on the advancement of one's own disability-related needs as opposed to the needs of a larger group. However, based on information known about all students, it may be possible to identify aspects of engaging in leadership activities that may be of particular challenge to students with LD. Initial engagement in new activities, and leadership activities in particular, can be a challenge for many students because of politics, lack of developed leadership skills, or the complexity of the position. On occasion, challenges with a leadership role are related specifically to a disability. For example, a student with ADHD may have difficulty with EF tasks necessary for a leadership position (e.g., long-term planning, balancing time demands of academic workload and the workload associated with the leadership position, maintaining attention during long meetings), whereas a student with LD may have difficulty writing reports or reviewing extensive minutes from prior meetings. However, disability-related challenges should not deter students from seeking and assuming leadership positions. Rather, students may need to be proactive in thinking about accommodations and strategies that will allow them to meet leadership obligations.

Some students with LD may have difficulty identifying and engaging in leadership activities and may need support to pursue them. For example, a student with ASD may be viewed by some faculty, staff, administrators, and students as incapable of holding a leadership position (e.g., a resident advisor or orientation leader) because of perceived limitations related to social interactions and communication. On the other hand, a student with ADHD may be viewed as an excellent candidate for an orientation leader position but may never complete the application as a result of difficulty activating (e.g., starting the application) and maintaining focus. Unfortunately, as has been discussed, a limitation associated with a disability constitutes only a single facet of the student's overall ability. A student with a disability may be highly qualified to serve in leadership positions on campus but may require accommodations, more accessible processes and procedures, or encouragement to do so. The variety of classroom accommodations presented in Chapter 4 can be, in many cases, adapted for use outside the classroom.

Student Conduct

The student conduct process is a means of holding students accountable to community expectations that support the educational mission of the institution. According to the Association for Student Conduct Administration (2016), the goals of the student conduct process are "student growth and development and the preservation of the educational environment" (¶2). Furthermore, conduct officers, those who uphold campus policies, "engage and educate students to be better citizens by guiding them towards ethical decision making and accountability" (Association for Student Conduct Administration, 2016, ¶2). Given the important role of these professionals in upholding campus values (e.g., safety, honesty, integrity) and the educational nature of their positions, these professionals need to be both proactive and reactive in their work with students. Although many students with LD will never engage in the student conduct system, some students will find themselves as complainants (i.e., making a claim that another student violated a policy) and others will find themselves as respondents (i.e., the person accused of violating a policy). Thus, conduct officers need to be prepared to work with students with LD to ensure that the discipline process is fully accessible.

It is common for campus policies to be presented to students as part of a first-year seminar, during orientation, or simply distributed as part of a student handbook. Often campus policies are dense, dull, and presented rather quickly over a short period of time. Although providing policy information is important, it is critical that the content is offered in multiple ways that are accessible to a wide range of learners. One consideration is to ensure that the vocabulary used in the policy is free of acronyms and jargon and not too advanced. Additionally, policies need to be presented in modalities that go beyond written text, such as videos, audio files, presentations, and discussions. To this end, faculty, staff, and administrators charged with imparting this information should ensure that the information is presented in a manner that adheres to UD principles.

As noted previously, for some students with ASD, policies and rules may need to be discussed one-to-one. Policies should be clear; ambiguity and subjectivity that result in shades of grey may be challenging for students who require greater certainty. If students with LD find themselves going through the conduct process at their institution, they should be provided with accessible conduct processes to ensure that they have the ability to participate fully and learn from the experience. As noted, an important goal of the student conduct process is student learning and development, so effective teaching strategies and philosophies should be employed. Planning and organization of conduct hearings, investigations, and interviews should be developed proactively in ways that align with UD. For example, questions should be asked clearly and directly using basic vocabulary and provided in multiple formats (e.g., verbally and in writing) and time for processing questions should be provided after questions have been asked. Students should have options for responding to questions (e.g., verbally or in written format). Another important consideration is ensuring that the climate of the conduct hearing is welcoming of students with LD. All conduct hearings should include formal notice to all students regarding the availability of accommodations.

When a student informs a conduct officer that they have LD, the conduct officer should refer the student to the appropriate office on campus (e.g., disability services) and consult with professionals in this office to ensure that the student is provided with necessary accommodations to be an active participant in the conduct process. Possible accommodations may include

- receipt of notes from the conduct hearing,
- use of technology for notetaking (e.g., laptop, tablet, smart pen),
- permission to audio record the hearing,
- readers or text-to-speech software, and
- breaks in the hearing process.

In some cases, a student with LD will need to receive a sanction for a violation of community standards that can be explained — but not excused — by the LD diagnosis. The question becomes, should they receive the same sanction that a student would if their behavior could not be explained by their LD? As noted by Livingston and colleagues (2013), "educators must work within the legal framework and the policy structures at their institutions in a manner that maximizes the flexibility of their interventions without undermining the consistency of the student conduct process" (p. 218). Essentially, consistency of policy enforcement and the conduct process are important, but latitude does exist. Livingston et al. (2013) highlighted that engaging with campus partners (e.g., disability services) may be one way to develop equitable sanctions that are student-centered and optimize student learning. To be clear, a disability does not excuse violating campus policies; however, it may help contextualize behaviors. Furthermore, understanding a student's disability may help a conduct officer identify services that would benefit the student (e.g., tutoring, health services, counseling).

Title IX Violations

Sexual violence, intimate partner violence, and stalking violate campus policies as well as state and, in some cases, federal law. According to Title IX of the Education Amendments of 1972 (20 U.S.C. § 1681 et seq.), "No person in the United States shall, on the basis of sex, be excluded from participation in, be denied the benefits of, or be subjected to discrimination under any education program or activity receiving Federal financial assistance." Furthermore, the Office of Civil Rights noted that "The sexual harassment of students, including sexual violence, interferes with students' right to receive an education free from discrimination and, in the case of sexual violence, is a crime" (Ali, 2011). Like any other college student, individuals with LD can be perpetrators or survivors of these crimes. All members of the campus community should take these crimes seriously. Policies and procedures for addressing these matters must be clear and shared with the entire institution in accordance with Title IX of the Education Amendments of 1972 (20 U.S.C. §1681 et seq.). Every individual on campus should be trained to support survivors of these crimes and should be aware of the laws and campus policies associated with reporting such crimes. A comprehensive, proactive plan for prevention and education regarding sexual violence, intimate partner violence, and stalking victimization must be in place. Colleges and universities must educate students about these crimes, the law, and associated campus policies in ways that are accessible and inclusive. As they are inside the classroom, UD principles should be used in the development of these critical educational programs so that no student is excluded. The cost of exclusion—particularly as it relates to education about these crimes—is far too great.

Across all students, rates of sexual violence, intimate partner violence, and stalking victimization are high. Tjaden and Thoennes (1998) defined stalking as "repeated visual or physical proximity, nonconsensual communication, or verbal, written or implied threats, or a combination thereof, that would cause a reasonable person fear" (p. 2). If they have challenges related to verbal and nonverbal communication, students with ASD or some other types of disabilities (e.g., closed head injury) may inadvertently direct communications or behaviors toward another person in ways that fit this definition. According to Williams (2016), stalking "is one of the most frequent charges that land a student with [ASD] in the conduct office" (p. 51). Unfortunately, some students with impaired communication skills may not recognize that these behaviors could cause someone to be fearful.

Brown, Peña, and Rankin (2017) found that college students with ASD and their peers with disabilities other than ASD are more likely to experience unwanted sexual contact than their peers without disabilities. Specifically, 4.6% of students without disabilities experienced unwanted sexual contact, compared with 8.2% of students with ASD and 9.3% of students with non-ASD disabilities (p. 773). Given the disproportionately high rates of unwanted sexual contact among students with disabilities, in particular students with ASD, faculty, staff, and administrators need to take additional efforts to educate and prepare students for the transition to college (Brown et al., 2017; Henry et al., 2010).

Moreover, sexual violence, intimate partner violence, and stalking victimization prevention and education programs that respect the differences in abilities, sexual orientations, social and personal experiences, and sex education are necessary. Students with LD would benefit from having content from presentations in written form as well as so that they can access the information fully. Although the use of slang and euphemism are common in authentic interactions, prevention and educational content should be presented explicitly and clearly to ensure students with LD benefit from prevention and education efforts.

Conclusion

Students with LD have and will continue to have the right to engage in all aspects of campus life, from academics to student life. Although many students with LD are engaged in campus life, others express that they have difficulty becoming involved. Thus, faculty, staff, and administrators coordinating out-of-class programs and services need to be aware of this often-overlooked population of students to ensure they are afforded full access and are welcomed participants in student life.

Chapter 6
Recommendations for Better Serving Students with LD

As noted, the vast majority of students who are eligible for services are not accessing them. Although some students with LD have developed compensatory strategies, attrition rates suggest that this is not the case for many (see Chapter 1). Therefore, it is worth considering what institutions of higher education can do to improve the outcomes and experiences of students who do not disclose their LD and students who do not have a formal diagnosis. In the remainder of this book, we look at six topics that are important to ensuring that diverse learners, particularly those with LD, are provided with an accessible education marked by inclusivity. These include disability-supportive campus climate, curricular and self-advocacy initiatives, programs for students with ASD, disability-related professional development and training, coaching services, and universal design.

Disability-Supportive Campus Climate

Although existing campus surveys assess disability climate in general (e.g., Stodden, Brown, & Roberts, 2011; Vogel, Holt, Sligar, & Leake, 2008), specific assessments of the climate for postsecondary students with learning disabilities are more elusive. If a college or university has a substantial population of identified students with LD, using institutional research resources to survey these students about their experience would be a starting point in assessing campus climate. Similarly, focus groups comprised of students with diverse learning profiles may provide a depth of understanding regarding the lived experiences of students.

Changing the campus mindset around disability issues should begin at the top with trustees, the president, and senior administrators making a commitment to improving access and inclusion for all faculty, staff, administrators, and students with disabilities. However, administrators frequently rely on the disability support services office to address access and inclusion issues without seeing disability issues as a campus-wide consideration (Brown & Broido, 2015). As a result, history demonstrates that change usually begins with grassroots efforts, advocacy, legislation, and lawsuits. Once a decision (or mandate) to change the culture around disability has been made, coordinated institutional efforts that span all offices (i.e., academic affairs, student life, human resources, admissions, institutional advancement) are necessary to improve climate (Harbour & Greenberg, 2017).

Still, Patton and Hannon (2008) noted the difficulty in campus-wide efforts to develop a more inclusive campus environment:

A major challenge in creating these cross-departmental collaborations is the unspoken and often unchallenged assumption that multicultural affairs offices or centers should bear the brunt of the responsibility for cultural education and programming. While such offices certainly have staff who are trained and skilled in this functional area, the responsibility of creating cross-cultural learning opportunities should be a collaborative one with various campus entities engaged in meaningful partnerships. (pp. 139-140)

This sentiment is also true of collaborations entered into by disability services offices. To be clear, disability services offices cannot be expected to change campus climate around disability single-handedly, nor should they be expected to provide all community-wide training. If campus climate is to change, all members of the campus community must come to the table ready to embrace, advocate, and contribute actively to the change. But what actions can be taken?

One way colleges and universities can work to improve disability-related campus climate is to address language. Although access is the goal of legislation to protect the rights of individuals with disabilities, institutions that move beyond compliance to creating a welcoming environment for all students should consider the words they use to describe ability and disability. In recent years, a number of institutions have renamed their disability services offices to place less emphasis on the word *disability* and more emphasis on the word *access*, in keeping with social models of disability. Thus, many offices once known as Disability Services are now the Office of Accessibility Services or the Center for Student Accessibility.

Additionally, many colleges and universities have embraced diversity initiatives to improve access and broaden the inclusion of their students. Neurodiversity can be incorporated into such initiatives, but attitudes regarding neurodiversity, and disability more broadly, as facets of diversity need to change. Growing up in the post-Civil Rights era, many first-year college students may be more knowledgeable of and comfortable with a broader definition of diversity than the faculty, staff, and administrators with whom they work. As it relates to disability, research indicates that students are quite willing to accept students with autism or intellectual disabilities on their campuses, often more willing than the faculty (Gibbons, Cihak, Mynatt, & Wilhoit, 2015). Although many faculty are willing to make minor accommodations for students with LD, they may balk at major accommodations or may simply be unaware of what is appropriate (Murray, Flannery, & Wren, 2008). Most faculty do not have substantial backgrounds in understanding LD and how to best accommodate students, but some research indicates that faculty training can greatly improve awareness and support for students with disabilities (Murray, Lombardi, & Wren, 2011).

A final suggestion to improve the disability-related climate of college and university campuses is to build on the idea that disability is a facet of diversity that should be celebrated.

Disability identity and disability culture are usually not celebrated and discussed on campuses in the same way that the cultures and identities of other traditionally marginalized student groups are. Although disability services professionals often will offer excellent campus programming on various disability-related topics, their primary job on campus is to ensure that students with disabilities are receiving needed accommodations. Unfortunately, opportunities to celebrate disability identity and culture are not immediate priorities.

In recent years, several colleges and universities have started to establish disability awareness and culture committees and sometimes even disability cultural centers to educate about and celebrate disability. Examples of institutions with such committees and cultural centers include Syracuse University, the University of Illinois Chicago, the University of North Carolina Asheville, and the University of Washington. Additionally, other institutions are beginning to develop on-campus neurodiversity centers (e.g., University of La Verne) and initiatives (e.g., The College of William and Mary) to highlight the experiences of individuals with diverse learning profiles as well as to disseminate information.

The federally funded Project Shift (http://www.projectshift-refocus.org/index.htm#intro) at Lane Community College included an examination of how disability can be reframed at the institutional level. The principal investigators identified a number of excellent suggestions for improving disability-related campus climate and is an excellent resource for institutions looking for ways to change practices. Notable project outcomes included the following:

- hosting discussions, events, and activities that promote disability culture;
- discontinuing the use of disability simulations;
- revising department literature and websites to reflect a social model of disability rather than a medical model of disability;
- expanding the Disability Support/Office of Accessibility mission statement to include playing a role in fostering an inclusive and welcoming campus community for individuals with disabilities; and
- increasing faculty consultation and outreach by establishing a faculty book club on disability, developing an ally program, and offering discussions of universal design (Funckes, Kroeger, Loewen, & Thornton, n.d.).

Climate change at the institutional level is never an easy task. In addition to clear differences in location, organizational structure, and size, individual colleges and universities differ in less apparent ways, such as in terms of their values, histories, and traditions. As such, efforts to change the climate around LD should be tailored to meet the needs of the individual college or university.

Curricular and Self-Advocacy Initiatives

Although pedagogical innovations can provide more access and improve learning for students with disabilities in numerous ways, changes in curriculum need to keep pace with evolving social perspectives and institutional values. Emerging from the disability rights movement, and in the same vein as other interdisciplinary area studies (e.g., African American studies, gender studies, Latin American studies), disability studies has been an academic discipline for more than two decades. Brueggemann (2013) discussed the intersection of disability culture, disability identity, and disability studies, noting that each evolved from myriad political, academic, and personal perspectives, but all in response to a medical model that promoted disability as pathological rather than as a naturally occurring difference. Syracuse University launched the first program of its kind in 1994, and as of 2016, 41 colleges and universities in North America offered degrees, minors, concentrations, or certificates in disability studies (Zubal-Ruggieri, 2016).

Although most colleges are not currently in a position to offer a disability studies program, incorporating discussion of disability into existing courses or creating standalone courses would provide students with entry points for discussions of disability. More important, such offerings would serve to acknowledge the lived experiences of a substantial number of students.

The development of self-advocacy skills is listed as an IEP goal for many K-12 students with LD, but students often arrive in higher education without the knowledge or skills to advocate for their own needs. At Landmark College, the unique educational environment provides opportunities to create curriculum focused on (a) developing students' self-understanding and knowledge of their individual LDs, (b) establishing an awareness of disability identity and its salience to the students, and (c) allowing students to practice self-advocacy skills. Landmark's required first-year seminar course, Perspectives in Learning, gives students an overview of all these areas while providing instruction on learning strategies and facilitating transition to the college. Students learn about the parts of the brain, information processing and memory systems, and components of executive functioning. Additionally, they practice a variety of strategies and systems for time management, note taking, active reading, and test taking. At the end of the semester, students demonstrate self-advocacy skills at a poster fair in which they discuss their own learning profiles and the specific strategies they find most beneficial. Although developing such a specific curriculum may not be appropriate for all institutions, providing opportunities for students to learn about their cognitive processes through scholarly perspectives on disability and civil rights can promote a more inclusive institutional mindset.

Other possible ways to support students with LD as they develop a sense of belonging and hone self-advocacy skills include establishing student study groups and offering study-skills workshops open to all students, not just those with LD. Providing tangible markers of institutional recognition of neurodiversity through films, book clubs, or scholarly activities can also demonstrate a positive and welcoming climate for those who learn differently. However, it is paramount to recognize that students with LD may or may not want to identify themselves as such; engagement in these groups and activities is a choice best left to the individual student.

Programs for Students with ASD

Increasingly, students on the autism spectrum are enrolling in college, but it is likely that many students who would meet the diagnostic criteria for ASD have successfully completed college and graduate school without ever having been diagnosed or having disclosed this difference. High-functioning individuals on the spectrum are becoming an increasingly familiar character type on popular television series (e.g., Sheldon on *The Big Bang Theory*, Max on *Parenthood*, and the protagonist on *The Good Doctor*). Whether dramatic or comedic in nature, these series portray individuals on the spectrum as odd, socially awkward, or literal-minded. Though media with limited understanding of ASD can exaggerate the social-pragmatic needs and savant-like strengths of individuals on the spectrum, it is clear that students with this profile may have significant challenges adjusting to the college environment, even when they are academically prepared. Gobbo and Shmulsky (2016) discussed the conflicting perspectives of the medical model and the autism acceptance model and suggested that postsecondary institutions recognize both perspectives, offering information on advocacy and helpful strategies to understand relative strengths and weaknesses of learners.

> It's extremely important for faculty, staff, and administrators to learn about autistic culture from actually autistic people! If there aren't any on your staff, there are myriad books, blogs, and #actuallyautistic Twitter feeds, among other things, so you can learn about autistic culture from the experts. True understanding is the key to empathetic service for autistic students. — *Sara Sanders Gardner, Autism Spectrum Navigators Program Director, Bellevue College*

Colleges and universities are recognizing the high achievement of many students on the spectrum and are attempting to identify support systems that may help. That said, such supports tend to be generic in nature rather than targeted to the social-pragmatic needs of individual students. In addition, most accommodations are academic in nature, and very few consider sensory issues or supports. In a study of community colleges, Brown and Coomes (2016) noted that only 26% were providing any services specific to students on the autism spectrum. More recently, in a sample of postsecondary institutions ($n = 469$), Brown (2017) found that 90% of institutions sampled used academically focused accommodations (e.g., extended exam time, note takers, alternative test sites), but 44.7% of institutions provided sensory accommodations and 28.3% of institutions offered ASD-specific services. Landmark College, due to its unique mission, offers a range of institutional supports for students with ASD, and many of these can be adapted to other institutions with a commitment and resources allocated to training and personnel (See Figure 6.1).

Programmatic Supports for Students with ASD

Early orientation: Voluntary pre-orientation programs can provide social adjustment and orientation to campus, residence hall, facilities, supports, and staff.

Parent involvement: Post-enrollment, family involvement can provide helpful information, including strategies. This contact has to be balanced with student independence and FERPA considerations.

Advising: Providing advisors with training specifically on ASD can be helpful. At Landmark College, several first-year student advisors have specialized certificate-level credentials.

Social-pragmatics groups: Planned social groups on campus as well as off-campus activities for interested students can help to develop a social cohort. These activities are facilitated by counselors or trained residential staff.

Leadership opportunities: Providing opportunities for students with ASD to get involved as peer mentors, orientation leaders, and other visible roles on campus can reduce stigma and improve student self-confidence.

Individualized program modifications: Students may have sensory issues or may request emotional support animals. Accessibility/disability support offices can provide significant support to students if students make contact early in the college enrollment process.

Figure 6.1. Programmatic supports for students with ASD (Shea & Donahue, 2017).

It is important to recognize that not all students with ASD will want or require services and that there is no one-size-fits-all model for program design. Primary goals should be reducing stigma, offering support, celebrating neurodiversity, and maintaining flexibility. Students on the spectrum are a heterogeneous group, and accommodations need to be specific and based on individual needs. Significantly, as Chapter 5 makes clear, the cocurricular program design and accommodations may be as important as the academic ones (Shea & Donahue, 2017).

Disability-Related Professional Development and Training

As has been discussed throughout this book, ensuring access and inclusion for students with LD is the responsibility of every member of a campus community, not just the disability services professionals. Unfortunately, most members of the faculty, staff, and administration lack preparation to serve students with disabilities (Kimball, Vaccaro, & Vargas, 2016; Murray et al., 2008; Sniatecki, Perry, & Snell, 2015).

Concerted efforts need to be made on the part of each higher education institution to ensure that their employees are sufficiently trained to work with students with diverse learning profiles. Offices including but not limited to disability services, equity and inclusion, and the provost, along with centers for teaching and learning, should advocate for such training. Collaboration among these offices is encouraged to ensure that ongoing professional development enhances employee understanding and skills related to serving students with LD. Recommended topics for trainings and workshops that can be offered by colleges and universities include

- executive functioning and the developing college student brain;
- services for students with disabilities, including counseling services and health services;
- appropriate referrals to disability services;
- philosophy of universal design as applied to course development, instruction, and assessment; and
- philosophy of universal design as applied to cocurricular and extracurricular activities.

Hands-on workshops, online training, brochures, scholarly presentations, and other methods of providing information and developing skills should be offered to meet the needs of diverse employees. In much the same way that students are varied in their learning profiles, so too are the profiles of faculty, staff, and administrators.

Graduate programs that prepare higher education faculty, staff, and administrators sometimes offer courses on teaching, learning, and diversity (Weisbuch & Cassuto, 2016). At a minimum, such courses should include information regarding variation in learning profiles, legal requirements, the importance of accommodations, accessible instructional strategies, and the philosophy of universal design. Additionally, these courses should provide opportunities to apply the disability-related content to authentic tasks (e.g., discussing disability-related topics with students; making appropriate referrals for services; and creating accessible courses, programs, materials, and assessments). As with professional development workshops, courses should model instructional practices that are accessible to diverse learners. For example, graduate courses and programs should be developed based on principles of universal design. Finally, courses on teaching, learning, and diversity should be components of all graduate training programs for future faculty and higher education professionals.

As college enrollment of students with diverse learning profiles increases, it is likely that individuals with LD are in the professional pipeline for every discipline. Efforts made to ensure that a high-quality and accessible education is afforded to all students in every discipline will serve to prepare future association members better. With this in mind, professional associations should encourage the exploration of accessible teaching methods appropriate to their specific disciplines and provide training and development opportunities that involve inclusive learning environments at local and national levels.

Finally, faculty, staff, and administrators need to identify avenues to enhance their own professional learning as it relates to serving students with LD. College and university employees need to move from passively acquiring information about disability if and when it is offered to actively seeking opportunities to develop the knowledge and skills needed to serve students with diverse learning profiles. Fortunately, employees at postsecondary institutions have indicated a desire to know more about students with disabilities (Murray et al., 2008; Murray et al., 2011; Murray, Wren, Stevens, & Keys, 2009), although they are uncertain how to obtain this information (Evans, Herriott, & Myers, 2009). This book, along with other available resources, can serve as a starting point for faculty, staff, and administrator professional development. Organizations with expertise in LD in higher education contexts include

- Association of Higher Education and Disability (AHEAD),
- College Autism Network (CAN),
- College Autism Spectrum (CAS),
- Landmark College Institute for Research and Training (LCIRT), and
- National Association of ADA Coordinators.

Coaching Services

Although research suggests that students with language-based LD, such as dyslexia, appear to benefit greatly from content-based tutoring and similar academic support, students with ADHD and EF challenges appear to derive the most benefit from coaching services (DuPaul, Dahlstrom-Hakki, et al., 2017). Executive function challenges are prevalent among college-aged students of all profiles due to the late maturation of brain regions that support self-regulation. Thus, coaching services can benefit a wide range of learners. We recommend that all colleges and universities either (a) implement coaching services on campus or (b) develop and make available a list of coaches in the surrounding community who have experience working with EF difficulties in young adults.

Coaching is usually delivered one-on-one at regularly scheduled meetings and check-ins with a person who is trained to support individuals with EF challenges (in particular students with ADHD). These coaches should understand the neurobiological underpinnings of ADHD and be well versed in effective approaches and strategies. Coaching is traditionally conducted in face-to-face meetings, but phone calls and video conferencing are becoming more common. In addition to regular meetings, coaches will often check in via text message, email, or phone calls to monitor a student's executive functioning. Given that this service goes beyond ensuring student access to the educational environment, some schools charge a separate fee for coaching.

Coaching differs from traditional campus supports such as content area tutoring, advising, and therapeutic counseling in several key ways. Coaches work collaboratively, in a nondirective fashion with their student-clients to address personal goals and needs. Unlike conventional tutoring, which focuses on content knowledge of particular courses and sometimes includes learning strategy instruction, coaching supports the development of skills, strategies, and beliefs needed to manage EF challenges such as planning, organizing, and activating to carry out tasks and assignments.

Above all, coaching fosters self-determination, defined by Field, Martin, Miller, Ward, and Wehmeyer (1998) as "a combination of skills, knowledge, and beliefs that enable a person to engage in goal-directed, self-regulated, autonomous behavior" (p. 2). This is achieved through the use of specific types of open-ended questions that "model reflective thinking and prompt students' ability to plan and carry out their goals" (Parker & Boutelle, 2009, p. 205). This questioning by the coach takes place throughout the duration of the goal-attainment cycle—planning, taking action, and reflecting on outcomes to modify subsequent approaches.

In a qualitative study, Parker and Boutelle (2009) found that students who participated in coaching were able to articulate how coaching supported their emerging autonomy while they learned how to develop and manage their EF skills. Students offered many positive assessments of coaching, including describing coaching as an equal partnership that required them to think and behave in new ways; noting that they felt more empowered to work autonomously toward personal goals; and indicating that coaching enhanced their overall well-being and helped them develop positive expectations about their futures (Parker & Boutelle, 2009).

Universal Design

Implementing a universal design (UD) approach to curriculum development and student services delivery is a broad-based way to meet the needs of students with diverse cognitive profiles while reducing the need for specialized, individual accommodations. The UD philosophy goes hand in hand with a social justice approach to disability, which reframes the construct of learning disability to that of cognitive diversity. UD not only anticipates but also welcomes a diversity of learners for their potential to enrich academic discourse, expanding the range of student perspectives and experiences on campus. Although a UD approach will not eliminate the need for accommodations mandated under Americans with Disabilities Act or Section 504 of the Rehabilitative Act, it is likely to reduce the number and extent of accommodations by front-loading accessibility and supports. Perhaps most important, UD has the potential to improve outcomes for all students, not just those with disabilities, by prompting educators, student services personnel, and administrators to consider which elements of curriculum or program are essential and which can be modified by providing options and scaffolding that will benefit the widest range of learners.

> 66
> Making a classroom more accessible never means dumbing down the material, as some people seem to think. Accessibility isn't about learning any less than a typical classroom teaches neurotypical students. It's about presenting the information in a way that different types of learners can understand. Every college should be working on making their curriculum more accessible. It's hard to see why they wouldn't want to; making a more accessible curriculum not only helps students with differences, but it helps the neurotypical students as well. — *Alicia* 99

Unlike the accommodations model, which identifies (and potentially stigmatizes) individuals based on their eligibility for disability services, the UD model meets the needs of students regardless of disability status. This includes the 75% of students identified with LD in grades K-12 who have chosen not to disclose their disability to college personnel (Horowitz et al., 2017) as well as those who have never been identified or who would not qualify for a diagnosis but nevertheless experience academic difficulty. Therefore, it serves the needs of students who are academically underprepared for a variety of reasons, including inadequate prior schooling, low socioeconomic status, chronic health issues, ESL status, and a variety of other categories.

Although research has not yet reached consensus on the validity of universal design (Faggella-Luby et al., 2017), the UD approach has been adopted broadly by a range of postsecondary institutions. Its early proponents at the University of Connecticut and the University of Washington's DO-IT Center published some of the first articles on the concept. Since that time Harvard University, Colorado State University, The George Washington University, University of Vermont, and Boston College, among others, have become advocates for implementing UD at the postsecondary level.

Faculty training in UD principles and practices is essential to implementation and has the added benefit of initiating discussions about effective teaching and learning in postsecondary settings, where faculty are generally focused more on content delivery than pedagogy. Successful models for faculty professional development include the Ensuring Access Through Collaboration and Technology (EnACT) program, developed to implement UD across several colleges throughout California via a faculty learning community, and the Florida Consortium on Postsecondary Education and Intellectual Disabilities, which developed an online instructional module for higher education faculty. Landmark College offers a five-course online certificate program in universal design for secondary and postsecondary educators, and the Landmark College Institute for Research and Training provides onsite or distance-based customized professional development on UD for schools and colleges. Additional resources for implementing UD principles in higher education settings include the following:

- Burgstahler, S. E. (2015). *Universal design of instruction (UDI): Definition, principles, guidelines, and examples.* Seattle, WA: University of Washington, DO-IT. Available at https://www.washington.edu/doit/universal-design-instruc-tion-udi-definition-principles-guidelines-and-examples

- Burgstahler, S. E., & Cory, R. C. (Eds.). (2010). *Universal design in higher education: From principles to practice.* Cambridge, MA: Harvard Educational Press.

- University of Connecticut FacultyWare (http://www.facultyware.uconn.edu/home.cfm)

- Center for Applied and Specialized Technology (CAST). (2018). *Universal design for learning guidelines* (Version 2.2). Retrieved from http://udlguidelines.cast.org

- National Center on Universal Design for Learning (http://www.udlcenter.org)

Conclusion

Postsecondary institutions have an opportunity and an obligation to address the barriers to access that impede the educational experience for students with disabilities. Despite the progress that has been made to increase access and inclusion of students with documented LD, substantial barriers still exist. It is the premise of this book that not only are there concrete steps that institutions can take to improve the outcomes and experiences of students with LD but that reducing barriers and stigma associated with disability benefits the broader campus community. Indeed, given the increasing number of students entering college who are underprepared for postsecondary education, it is imperative that institutions identify and adopt strategies and philosophies that benefit all learners. With such access, we believe that graduation rates will improve. Students with LD can and do contribute to the academic scholarship and the communities of the postsecondary institutions they join. We celebrate the diversity that all learners bring to the table and look forward to the contributions each can make when given the opportunity.

REFERENCES

ADHD Institute. (2017). *Heritability*. Retrieved from http://adhd-institute.com/burden-of-adhd/aetiology/heritability/

Ali, R. (2011). *Dear colleague letter: Sexual violence*. Washington, DC: U.S. Department of Education, Office for Civil Rights. Retrieved from http://www2.ed.gov/about/offices/list/ocr/letters/colleague-201104.html

Alpern, C. S., & Zager, D. (2007). Addressing communication needs of young adults with autism in a college-based inclusion program. *Education and Training in Developmental Disabilities, 42*, 428-436.

Altman, B. (2001). Disability definitions, models, classification schemes, and applications. In G. L. Albrecht, K. Seelman, & M. Bury (Eds.), *Handbook of disability studies* (pp. 97-122). Thousand Oaks, CA: Sage.

American Psychiatric Association. (2013). *Diagnostic and statistical manual of mental disorders* (5th ed.). Washington, DC: Author.

Americans with Disabilities Act Amendments Act of 2008. Pub. L. No. 110-325, 42 U.S.C. §§ 12101 et seq. (2008).

Archer, D. (2014, May 14). ADHD: The entrepreneur's superpower. *Forbes*. Retrieved from http://www.forbes.com/

Association for Student Conduct Administration. (2016). *Frequently asked questions*. Retrieved from http://www.theasca.org/faq

Astin, A. W. (1993). *What matters in college: Four critical years revisited*. San Francisco, CA: Jossey-Bass.

Astin, A. W. (1999). Student involvement: A developmental theory for higher education. *Journal of College Student Development, 40*, 518-529.

Baio, J., Wiggins., L., Christensen, D. L., Maenner, M. J., Daniels, J., Warren, Z., ... Dowling, N. F. (2018). Prevalence of autism spectrum disorder among children aged 8 years — Autism and Developmental Disabilities Monitoring Network, 11 sites, United States, 2014. *Morbidity and Mortality Weekly Report Surveillance Summaries, 67*(6),1-23. https://doi.org/10.15585/mmwr.ss6706a1

Ballou, R., Reavill, L., & Schultz, B. (1995). Assessing the immediate and residual effects of the residence hall experience: Validating Pace's 1990 study of on-campus and off campus students. *Journal of College and University Student Housing, 25*, 16-21.

Banks, J. (2014). Barriers and supports to postsecondary transition: Case studies of African American students with disabilities. *Remedial and Special Education, 35*(1), 28-39.

Barkley, R. A. (1997). *ADHD and the nature of self-control*. New York, NY: Guilford.

Barkley, R. A. (1998). Attention-deficit hyperactivity disorder. *Scientific American, 279*(3), 44-49.

Barkley, R. A. (2004, April). *Attention deficit disorder.* Presentation at Landmark College, Putney, VT.

Barkley, R. A. (2010). Deficient emotional self-regulation is a core component of ADHD. *Journal of ADHD and Related Disorders, 1,* 5-37.

Barkley, R. A., & Murphy, K. R. (2011). The nature of executive function (EF) deficits in daily life activities in adults with ADHD and their relationship to performance on EF tests. *Journal of Psychopathology and Behavioral Assessment, 33*(2), 137-158. https://doi.org/10.1007/s10862-011-9217-x

Barnett, J. P., & Maticka-Tyndale, E. (2015). Qualitative exploration of sexual experiences among adults on the autism spectrum: Implications for sex education. *Perspectives on Sexual and Reproductive Health, 47*(4), 171-179.

Batorowicz, B., Missiuna, C. A., & Pollock, N. A. (2012). Technology supporting written productivity in children with learning disabilities: A critical review. *Canadian Journal of Occupational Therapy, 79*(4), 211-224.

Bennett, A., Tomkinson, M., & Miller, J. (2015). *Why is it so hard for someone with autism to make eye contact?* [Blog post]. Retrieved from https://www.autismspeaks.org/blog/2015/07/17/why-it-so-hard-someone-autism-make-eye-contact

Berger, I., Slobodin, O., Aboud, M., Melamed, J., & Cassuto, H. (2013). Maturational delay in ADHD: Evidence from CPT. *Frontiers in Human Neuroscience, 7,* 1-11.

Berninger, V., Nielsen, K., & Raskind, W. (2008). Writing problems in developmental dyslexia: Under-recognized and undertreated. *Journal of School Psychology, 46*(1), 1-46.

Biederman, J., Ball, S. W., Monuteaux, M. C., Surman, C. B., Johnson, J. L., & Zeitlin, S. (2007). Are girls with ADHD at risk for eating disorders? Results from a controlled, five-year prospective study. *Journal of Developmental and Behavioral Pediatrics, 28*(4), 302-307.

Biederman, J., Monuteaux, M. C., Spencer, T., Wilens, T. E., MacPherson, H. A., & Faraone, S. V. (2008). Stimulant therapy and risk for subsequent substance use disorders in male adults with ADHD: A naturalistic controlled 10-year follow-up study. *American Journal of Psychiatry, 165*(5), 597-603.

Bishop, D. V., & Snowling, M. J. (2004). Developmental dyslexia and specific language impairment: Same or different? *Psychological Bulletin, 130*(6), 858-886.

Brown, K., & Broido, E. (2015). Engaging students with disabilities. In S. R. Harper & S. J. Quaye (Eds.), *Student engagement in higher education: Theoretical perspectives and practical approaches for diverse populations* (2nd ed., pp. 188-207). New York, NY: Routledge.

Brown, K. R. (2017). Accommodations and support services for students with autism spectrum disorder (ASD): A national survey of disability resource providers. *Journal of Postsecondary Education and Disability, 30*(2), 141-156.

Brown, K. R., & Coomes, M. D. (2016). A spectrum of support: Current and best practices for students with Autism Spectrum Disorder (ASD) at community colleges. *Community College Journal of Research and Practice, 40*(6), 465-479. https://doi.org/10.1080/1 0668926.2015.1067171

Brown, K. R., Peña, E. V., & Rankin, S. (2017). Unwanted sexual contact: Students with autism and other disabilities at greater risk. *Journal of College Student Development, 58*(5), 771-776.

Brown, L. (2011). *Identity-first language.* Retrieved from http://autisticadvocacy.org/about-asan/identity-first-language/

Brown, T. E. (2005). *Attention deficit disorder: The unfocused mind in children and adults.* New Haven, CT: Yale University.

Brown Clinic. (n.d.). *The Brown model of ADD/ADHD.* Retrieved from http://www.brown-adhdclinic.com/add-adhd-model/

Brueggemann, B. (2013). Disability studies/disability culture. In M. L. Wehmeyer (Ed.), *The Oxford handbook of positive psychology and disability* (pp. 279-299). New York, NY: Oxford University Press. https://doi.org/10.1093/oxfordhb/9780195398786.013.013.0019

Bureau of Labor Statistics, U. S. Department of Labor. (2013, April 24). *Persons with a disability: Barriers to employment, types of assistance, and other labor-related issues summary* [Press release]. Retrieved from https://www.bls.gov/news.release/dissup.nr0.htm

Busby, R. R., Gammel, H. L., & Jeffcoat, N. K. (2002). Grades, graduation, and orientation: A longitudinal study of how new student programs relate to grade point average and graduation. *Journal of College Orientation and Transition, 10*(1), 45-57.

Cameto, R., Levine, P., & Wagner, M. (2004). *Transition planning for students with disabilities.* A special topic report from the National Longitudinal Transition Study-2 (NLTS2). Menlo Park, CA: SRI International.

Centers for Disease Control and Prevention (CDC). (2016). *Autism spectrum disorder (ASD).* Retrieved from https://www.cdc.gov/ncbddd/autism/data.html

Centers for Disease Control and Prevention (CDC). (2017). *Physical activity facts.* Retrieved from https://www.cdc.gov/healthyschools/physicalactivity/facts.htm

Chickering, A. W., & Reisser, L. (1993). *Education and identity* (2nd ed.). San Francisco, CA: Jossey-Bass.

Chickering, A. W., & Schlossberg, N. (1995). *Getting the most out of college.* Needham Heights, MA: Allyn & Bacon.

Clark, M., & Parette, P. (2002). Student athletes with learning disabilities: A model for effective supports. *College Student Journal, 36*(1), 47-62.

Cole, E., & Cawthon, S. (2015). Self-disclosure decisions of university students with learning disabilities. *Journal of Postsecondary Education and Disability, 28*(2), 163-179.

Cortiella, C., & Horowitz, S. H. (2014). *The state of learning disabilities: Facts, trends, and emerging issues* (3rd ed.). New York, NY: National Center for Learning Disabilities. Retrieved from http://www.ncld.org/wp-content/uploads/2014/11/2014-State-of-LD.pdf

Cowan, N. (2010). The magical mystery four: How is working memory capacity limited, and why? *Current Issues in Psychological Science, 19*(1), 51-57. Retrieved from https://www.ncbi.nlm.nih.gov/pmc/articles/PMC2864034/

Croteau, J. M., & Talbot, D. M. (2000). Understanding the landscape: An empirical view of lesbian, gay, and bisexual issues in the student affairs profession. In V. A. Wall & N. J. Evans (Eds.), *Toward acceptance: Sexual orientation and today's college campus* (pp. 3-28). Lanham, MD: University Press of America.

CUNY Council on Student Disability Issues. (2014). *Reasonable accommodations: A faculty guide to teaching students with disabilities.* Retrieved from http://www.ccny.cuny.edu/sites/default/files/2014-Reasonable-Accommodations-Faculty-Guide-to-Teaching-Students-with-Disabilities.pdf

Dalton, J. C., & Crosby, P. C. (2012). Reinventing the extracurriculum: The educational and moral purposes of college student activities and experiences. *Journal of College and Character, 13*(3), 1-7.

D'Arcangelo, M. (2001). Wired for mathematics: A conversation with Brian Butterworth. *Educational Leadership, 59*(3), 14-19.

DeFreitas, T. (2018, January 24). *College to career transition: Leveraging the ADA & accommodations at work* [Webinar]. Retrieved from https://askjan.org/landingpage/AHEAD-Jan2018/

Desroches, A. S., Joanisse, M. F., & Robertson, E. K. (2006). Specific phonological impairments in dyslexia revealed by eyetracking. *Cognition, 100*(3), B32-B42.

Dolmage, J. T. (2014). *Disability rhetoric.* Syracuse, NY: Syracuse University Press.

Dolmage, J. T. (2017). *Academic ableism: Disability and higher education.* Ann Arbor, MI: University of Michigan.

Dunn, D. S., & Andrews, E. E. (2015). Person-first and identity-first language: Developing psychologists' cultural competence using disability language. *American Psychologist, 70*(3), 255-264.

Dunn, P. A. (2001). *Talking, sketching, moving: Multiple literacies in the teaching of writing.* Portsmouth, NH: Boynton/Cook Heinemann.

DuPaul, G. J., Dahlstrom-Hakki, I., Gormley, M. J., Fu, Q., Pinho, T. D., & Banerjee, M. (2017). College students with ADHD and LD: Effects of support services on academic performance. *Learning Disabilities Research & Practice, 32*(4), 246-256.

DuPaul, G. J., Pinho, T. D., Pollack, B. L., Gormley, M. J., & Laracy, S. D. (2017). First-year college students with ADHD and/or LD: Differences in engagement, positive core self-evaluation, school preparation, and college expectations. *Journal of Learning Disabilities, 50*(3), 238-251.

Dyer, N. A. (2008). Inclusive advising: Building competencies to better serve students with disabilities. *Academic Advising Today, 31*(3). Retrieved from https://www.nacada.ksu.edu/Resources/Academic-Advising-Today.aspx

Dyscalculia.org. (n.d.a). *College and dyscalculia.* Retrieved from http://www.dyscalculia.org/college-dyscalculia

Dyscalculia.org. (n.d.b). *Dyscalculia checklist.* Retrieved from http://www.dyscalculia.org/diagnosis-legal-matters/math-ld-symptoms

Ebert-May, D., Brewer, C., & Allred, S. (1997). Innovation in large lectures—teaching for active learning. *BioScience, 47*(9), 601-607.

Eide, B. L., & Eide, F. F. (2012). *The dyslexic advantage: Unlocking the hidden potential of the dyslexic brain.* New York, NY: Penguin.

Eide, F. (2015, September). *Why reading with dyslexia is easier on your phone.* Retrieved from https://www.dyslexicadvantage.org/why-reading-with-dyslexia-is-easier-on-your-phone/

Evans, N., Assadi, J., & Herriott, T. (2005). Encouraging the development of disability allies. In R. Reason, E. Broido, T. Davis, & N. Evans (Eds.), *Developing social justice allies* (New Directions for Student Services, No. 110, pp. 67-79). San Francisco, CA: Jossey-Bass.

Evans, N., Broido, E., Brown, K., & Wilke, A. (2017). *Disability in higher education: A social justice approach.* San Francisco, CA: Jossey-Bass.

Evans, N. J., Herriott, T. K., & Myers, K. A. (2009). Integrating disability into the diversity framework in the training of student affairs professionals. In J. L. Higbee & A. A. Mitchell (Eds.), *Making good on the promise: Student affairs professionals with disabilities* (pp. 111-128). Lanham, MD: University Press of America.

Faggella-Luby, M., Dukes III, L. L., Gelbar, N., Madaus, J. W., Lombardi, A., & Lalor, A. (2017). Universal design and college students with disabilities: Does the data equal the zeal? *Currents in Teaching and Learning, 9,* 5-19.

Fiedorowicz, C., Benezra, E., MacDonald, W., McElgunn, B., Wilson, A., & Kaplan, B. (2001). Neurobiological basis of learning disabilities: An update. *Learning Disabilities—Multidisciplinary Journal, 11*(2), 61-74.

Field, S., Martin, J., Miller, R., Ward, M., & Wehmeyer, M. (1998). *A practical guide for teaching self-determination.* Reston, VA: Council for Exceptional Children.

Frye, D. (n.d.). What does dyscalculia look like in adults? *ADDitude Magazine.* Retrieved from https://www.additudemag.com/

Fujiura, G., & Rutkowski-Kmitta, V. (2001). Counting disability. In G. L. Albrecht, K. Seelman, & M. Bury (Eds.), *Handbook of disability studies* (pp. 69-96). Thousand Oaks, CA: Sage.

Funckes, C., Kroeger, S., Loewen, G., & Thornton, M. (n.d.). *Refocus: Viewing the work of disability services differently.* Retrieved from http://www.projectshift-refocus.org/index.htm

Ganschow, L., Sparks, R. L., & Javorsky, J. (1998). Foreign language learning difficulties: An historical perspective. *Journal of Learning Disabilities, 31*(3), 248-258.

Gelbar, N. W., Shefcyk, A., & Reichow, B. (2015). A comprehensive survey of current and former college students with autism spectrum disorders. *The Yale Journal of Biology and Medicine, 88*, 45-68.

Geschwind, N. (1984). The brain of a learning-disabled individual. *Annals of Dyslexia, 34*(1), 319-327.

Gibbons, M., Cihak, D., Mynatt, B., & Wilhoit, B. (2015). Faculty and student attitudes toward postsecondary education for students with intellectual disabilities and autism. *Journal of Postsecondary Education and Disability, 28*(2), 149-162.

Gibson, J. (2006). Disability and clinical competency: An introduction. *The California Psychologist, 39*, 6-10.

Gill, C. J. (1997). Four types of integration in disability identity development. *Journal of Vocational Rehabilitation, 9*, 39-46.

Gobbo, K., & Shmulsky, S. (2014). Faculty experience with college students with autism spectrum disorders: A qualitative study of challenges and solutions. *Focus on Autism and Other Developmental Disabilities, 29*(1), 13-22.

Gobbo, K., & Shmulsky, S. (2016). Autistic identity development and postsecondary education. *Disability Studies Quarterly, 36*(3). Retrieved from http://dsq-sds.org/article/view/5053/4412

Grandin, T. (2014, September 4). *Different kinds of minds.* Speech presented at Landmark College, Putney, VT.

Gregg, N. (2007). Underserved and unprepared: Postsecondary learning disabilities. *Learning Disabilities Research & Practice, 22*(4), 219-228.

Hadley, W. M. (2007). The necessity of academic accommodations for first-year college students with learning disabilities. *Journal of College Admission, 195*, 9-13.

Hadley, W. M. (2011). College students with disabilities: A student development perspective. In W. S. Harbour & J. W. Madaus (Eds.), *Disability services and campus dynamics* (New Directions for Higher Education, No. 154, pp. 77-81). San Francisco, CA: Jossey-Bass.

Haegele, J.A., & Hodge, S. (2016). Disability discourse: Overview and critiques of the medical and social models. *Quest, 68*, 193-206.

Haft, S. L., & Hoeft, F. (2016, December). *What protective factors lead to resilience in students with dyslexia?* Retrieved from https://dyslexiaida.org/what-protective-factors-lead-to-resilience-in-students-with-dyslexia/

Hall, S. L., Scott, F., & Borsz, M. (2008). A constructivist case study examining the leadership development of undergraduate students in campus recreational sports. *Journal of College Student Development, 49*(2), 125-140.

Harbour, W. S., & Greenberg, D. (2017, July). Campus climate and students with disabilities. *NCCSD Research Brief, 1*(2), 139-140. Retrieved from http://www.NCCSDonline.org

Hartman-Hall, H. M., & Haaga, D. A. (2002). College students' willingness to seek help for their learning disabilities. *Learning Disability Quarterly, 25*(4), 263-274.

Haynie, D. (2014, April 4). Students with disabilities meet challenges in online courses. *U.S. News & World Report.* Retrieved from https://www.usnews.com/

HEATH Resource Center. (n.d.). *Students with autism in the college classroom.* Retrieved from https://www.heath.gwu.edu/students-autism-college-classroom

Hecker, L. (1997). Walking, tinkertoys, and Legos: Using movement and manipulatives to help students write. *The English Journal, 86*(6), 46-52.

Hecker, L., Burns, L., Katz, L., Elkind, J., & Elkind, K. (2002). Benefits of assistive reading software for students with attention disorders. *Annals of Dyslexia, 52*(1), 243-272.

Hecker, L., & Fein, A. M. (2014, April). Digital note-taking: Helping you get it and keep it together. *Attention Magazine.* Retrieved from http://www.chadd.org/Membership/Attention-Magazine/Attention-Magazine-Article.aspx?id=2

Hedrick, B., Dizén, M., Collins, K., Evans, J., & Grayson, T. (2010). Perceptions of college students with and without disabilities and effects of STEM and non-STEM enrollment on student engagement and institutional involvement. *Journal of Postsecondary Education and Disability, 23*(2), 129-136.

Henry, W. J., Fuerth, K., & Figliozzi, J. (2010). Gay with a disability: A college student's multiple cultural journey. *College Student Journal, 44*(2), 377-388.

Higbee, J. L., & Eaton, S. B. (2008). Implementing Universal Design in learning centers. In J. L. Higbee & E. Goff (Eds.), *Pedagogy and student services for institutional transformation: Implementing universal design in higher education* (pp. 217-224). Minneapolis, MN: College of Education and Human Development, University of Minneapolis. Retrieved from http://cehd.umn.edu/passit/docs/PASS-IT-BOOK.pdf

Hill, K. M. (2016). A social constructivist model of teacher knowledge: The PCK of biology faculty at a large research university. In G. Weaver, W. Burgess, A. Childress, & L. Slakey (Eds.), *Transforming institutions: 21st century undergraduate STEM education* (pp. 353-368). West Lafayette, IN: Purdue University.

Horowitz, S. H., Rawe, J., & Whittaker, M. C. (2017). *The state of learning disabilities: Understanding the 1 in 5.* New York, NY: National Center for Learning Disabilities. Retrieved from https://www.ncld.org/the-state-of-learning-disabilities-understanding-the-1-in-5

Howland, C. L., & Gibavic, E. (2013). Learning disability identity development and social construct: A two-tiered approach. In M. Adams, W. J. Blumengeld, D. Chase, J. Catalano, K. Dejong, H. W. Hackman, … X. Zuniga (Eds.), *Readings for diversity and social justice* (pp. 522-528). New York, NY: Taylor & Francis.

Individuals with Disabilities Education Act, 20 U.S.C. § 1400 (2004).

International Dyslexia Association. (n.d.a). *Dyslexia and the brain*. Retrieved from https://dyslexiaida.org/dyslexia-basics/

International Dyslexia Association. (n.d.b). *Dyslexia basics*. Retrieved from https://dyslexiaida.org/dyslexia-basics/

Jones, S., & Abes, E. (2013). *Identity development of college students: Advancing frameworks for multiple dimensions of identity*. San Francisco, CA: Jossey-Bass.

Kelly, R. (2010, July 22). Teaching students with learning disabilities in the online classroom. *Faculty Focus*. Retrieved from https://www.facultyfocus.com

Kennedy, K., & Upcraft, M. L. (2010). Keys to student success: A look at the literature. In M. S. Hunter, B. F. Tobolowsky, J. N. Gardner, S. E. Evenbeck, J. A. Pattengale, … L. A. Schreiner (Eds.), *Helping sophomores succeed: Understanding and improving the second-year experience* (pp. 30-42). San Francisco, CA: Jossey-Bass.

Kerschbaum, S., Eisenman, L., & Jones, J. (Eds.). (2017). *Negotiating disability: Disclosure and higher education*. Ann Arbor, MI: University of Michigan Press. https://doi.org/10.3998/mpub.9426902

Kessler, R. C., Adler, L., Barkley, R., Biederman, J., Conners, C. K., Demler, O., ... Spencer, T. (2006). The prevalence and correlates of adult ADHD in the United States: Results from the National Comorbidity Survey replication. *American Journal of Psychiatry, 163*(4), 716-723.

Keup, J. R., Gahagan, J., & Goodwin, R. (2010). *2008 national survey of sophomore-year initiatives: Curricular and co-curricular structures supporting the success of second-year college students* (Research Reports on College Transitions No. 1). Columbia, SC: University of South Carolina, National Resource Center for The First-Year Experience & Students in Transition.

Kim, J., & Bastedo, M. N. (2016). Athletics, clubs, or music? The influence of college extracurricular activities on job prestige and satisfaction. *Journal of Education and Work, 30*(3), 249-269.

Kimball, E., Vaccaro, A., & Vargas, N. (2016). Student affairs professionals supporting students with disabilities: A grounded theory model. *Journal of Student Affairs Research and Practice, 53*(2), 175-189.

Kinzie, J. (2013). Taking stock of capstones and integrated learning. *Peer Review, 15*(4), 27-30.

Kolb, B., Gibb, R., & Robinson, T. (2003). Brain plasticity and behavior. *Current Directions in Psychological Science, 12*(1), 1-5. https://doi.org/10.1111/1467-8721.01210

Kornasky, L. (2009). Identity politics and invisible disability in the classroom. *Inside Higher Ed*. https://www.insidehighered.com/views/2009/03/17/identity-politics-and-invisible-disability-classroom

Komives, S. R., Owen, J. E., Longerbeam, S. D., Mainella, F. C., & Osteen, L. (2005). Developing a leadership identity: A grounded theory. *Journal of College Student Development, 46*(6), 593-611.

Kuh, G. D. (2008). *High-impact educational practices: What they are, who has access to them, and why they matter.* Washington, DC: Association of American Colleges and Universities.

Lalor, A. R. (2017). *Identification of disability-related competencies for student affairs generalists: A Delphi study* (Doctoral dissertation). Retrieved from http://digitalcommons.uconn.edu/dissertations/1346

Lalor, A. R., & Madaus, J. W. (2013). Helping students with disabilities search for colleges: Tips for professionals. *Insights on Learning Disabilities, 10*(1), 53-72.

Learning Disabilities Association of America (n.d.a). *Dyscalculia.* Retrieved from https://ldaamerica.org/types-of-learning-disabilities/dyscalculia/

Learning Disabilities Association of America. (n.d.b). *Graphic organizers.* Retrieved from https://ldaamerica.org/graphic-organizers/

Learning Disabilities Association of America. (n.d.c). *New to LD.* Retrieved from https://ldaamerica.org/support/new-to-ld/

Livingston, W. G., Scott, D. A., Rush, S. B., Watson, L. A., Neiduski, M. L., & Pinkenburg, S. J. (2013). When community and conduct collide: Residents with invisible disabilities and the student conduct process. *Journal of College & University Student Housing, 40*(1), 214-227.

Lombardi, A. R., & Lalor, A. R. (2017). Faculty and administrator knowledge and attitudes regarding disability: A review and a call for action. In E. Kim & K. C. Aquino (Eds.), *Disability as diversity in higher education: Policies and practices to advance student success* (pp. 107-121). New York, NY: Routledge.

MacArthur, C. (2009). Reflections on research on writing and technology for struggling writers. *Learning Disabilities Research & Practice, 24*(2), 93-103.

Madaus, J. W. (2005). Navigating the college transition maze: A guide for students with learning disabilities. *Teaching Exceptional Children, 37*(3), 32-37.

Madaus, J. W. (2006). Improving the transition to career for college students with learning disabilities: Suggestions from graduates. *Journal of Postsecondary Education and Disability, 19*(1), 85-93.

Madaus, J. W., McKeown, K., Gelbar, N., & Banerjee, M. (2012). The online and blended learning experience: Differences for students with and without learning disabilities and attention deficit/hyperactivity disorder. *International Journal for Research in Learning Disabilities, 1*(1), 21-36.

Madaus, J. W., Scott, S., & McGuire, J. (2003). *Barriers and bridges to learning as perceived by postsecondary students with learning disabilities* (Technical Report No. 01). Storrs, CT: University of Connecticut, Center on Postsecondary Education and Disability.

Mamiseishvili, K., & Koch, L. C. (2011). First-to-second-year persistence of students with disabilities in postsecondary institutions in the United States. *Rehabilitation Counseling Bulletin, 54*(2), 93-105.

Marshak, L., Van Wieren, T., Ferrell, D. R., Swiss, L., & Dugan, C. (2010). Exploring barriers to college student use of disability services and accommodations. *Journal of Postsecondary Education and Disability, 22*(3), 151-165.

McFarland, J., Hussar, B., de Brey, C., Snyder, T., Wang, X., Wilkinson-Flicker, S., ... Bullock Mann, F. (2017). *The condition of education 2017*. NCES 2017-144. Washington, DC: National Center for Education Statistics.

McGuire, J., Scott, S., & Shaw, S. (2006). Universal design and its applications in educational environments. *Remedial and Special Education, 27*(3), 166-175.

Meade-Kelly, V. (2013, February). *New research investigates inherited causes of autism* [Press release]. Retrieved from https://www.broadinstitute.org/news/4624

Meaux, J. B., Green, A., & Broussard, L. (2009). ADHD in the college student: A block in the road. *Journal of Psychiatric and Mental Health Nursing, 16*, 248-256.

Molina, B. S., Flory, K., Hinshaw, S. P., Greiner, A. R., Arnold, L. E., Swanson, J. M., ... Pelham, W. E. (2007). Delinquent behavior and emerging substance use in the MTA at 36 months: Prevalence, course, and treatment effects. *Journal of the American Academy of Child & Adolescent Psychiatry, 46*(8), 1028-1040.

Mooney, J., & Cole, D. (2000). *Learning outside the lines: Two Ivy League students with learning disabilities and ADHD give you the tools for academic success and educational revolution*. New York, NY: Simon & Schuster.

Morgan, P. L, Farkas, G., Hillemeier, M. M., Mattison, R., Maczuga, S., Li, H., & Cook, M. (2015). Minorities are disproportionately underrepresented in special education: Longitudinal evidence across five disability conditions. *Educational Researcher, 44*(5), 278-292. https://doi.org/10.3102/0013189X15591157

Morris, K., Frechette, C., Dukes, L., III, Stowell, N., Topping, N., & Brodosi, D. (2016). Closed captioning matters: Examining the value of closed captions for "all" students. *Journal of Postsecondary Education and Disability, 29*(3), 231-238.

Murray, C., Flannery, B. K., & Wren, C. (2008). University staff members' attitudes and knowledge about learning disabilities and disability support services. *Journal of Postsecondary Education and Disability, 21*(2), 73-90.

Murray, C., Lombardi, A., & Wren, C. T. (2011). The effects of disability-focused training on the attitudes and perceptions of university staff. *Remedial and Special Education, 32*(4), 290-300.

Murray, C., Wren, C. T., Stevens, E. B., & Keys, C. (2009). Promoting university faculty and staff awareness of students with learning disabilities: An overview of the Productive Learning u Strategies (PLuS) project. *Journal of Postsecondary Education and Disability, 22*(2), 117-129.

Myers, K. A. (2009). A new vision for disability education: Moving on from the add-on. *About Campus, 14*(5), 15-21.

Myers, K. A. (2017). [Review of the book Disability in higher education: A social justice approach by N. J. Evans, E. M. Broido, K. R. Brown, & A. K. Wilke]. *Journal of College Student Development, 58*(5), 792-794.

Myers, K. A., & Bastian, J. J. (2010). Understanding communication preferences of college students with visual disabilities. *Journal of College Student Development, 51*, 265-278. https://doi.org/10.1353/csd.0.0129

Myers, K. A., Lindburg, J. J., & Nied, D. M. (2014). Allies for inclusion: Disability and equity in higher education. *ASHE Higher Education Report, 39*, 1-132. https://doi.org/10.1002/aehe.20011

Nagi, S. (1965). Some conceptual issues in disability and rehabilitation. In M. B. Sussman (Ed.), *Sociology and rehabilitation* (pp. 100-113). Washington, DC: American Sociological Association.

National Institutes of Health. (2017). *Autism spectrum disorder.* Retrieved from https://ghr.nlm.nih.gov/condition/autism-spectrum-disorder#genes

National Survey of Student Engagement. (2017). *Engagement insights: Survey findings on the quality of undergraduate education—Annual Results 2017.* Bloomington, IN: Indiana University Center for Postsecondary Research. Retrieved from http://nsse.indiana.edu/html/annual_results.cfm

Newman, L. A., & Madaus, J. W. (2015a). Analysis of factors related to receipt of accommodations and services by postsecondary students with disabilities. *Remedial and Special Education, 36*(4), 208-219.

Newman, L. A., & Madaus, J. W. (2015b). Reported accommodations and supports provided to secondary and postsecondary students with disabilities: National perspective. *Career Development and Transition for Exceptional Individuals, 38*(3), 173-181.

Newman, L. A., Madaus, J., & Javitz, H. (2016). Effect of transition planning activities on postsecondary support receipt by students with disabilities. *Exceptional Children, 82*(4), 497-514.

Newman, L. A., Madaus, J. W., Lalor, A. R., & Javitz, H. S. (in press). Support receipt: Effect on postsecondary success of students with learning disabilities. *Career Development and Transition for Exceptional Individuals.*

Newman, L., Wagner, M., Cameto, R., Knokey, A.-M., & Shaver, D. (2010). *Comparisons across time of the outcomes of youth with disabilities up to 4 years after high school. A report of findings from the National Longitudinal Transition Study (NLTS) and the National Longitudinal Transition Study-2 (NLTS2)* (NCSER 2010-3008). Menlo Park, CA: SRI International.

Newman, L., Wagner, M., Knokey, A., Marder, C., Nagle, K. Shaver, D., & Wei, X. (2011). *The post-high school outcomes of young adults with disabilities up to 8 years after high school: A report from the National Longitudinal Transition Study-2 (NLTS2)* (NCSER 2011-3005). Menlo Park, CA: SRI International.

Nilson, L., & Zimmerman, B. (2013). *Creating self-regulated learners.* Sterling, VA: Stylus.

Oseguera, L., & Rhee, B. S. (2009). The influence of institutional retention climates on student persistence to degree completion: A multilevel approach. *Research in Higher Education, 50*(6), 546-569.

Parker, D. R., & Boutelle, K. (2009). Executive function coaching for college students with learning disabilities and ADHD: A new approach for fostering self-determination. *Learning Disabilities Research & Practice, 24*(4), 204-215.

Pascarella, E. T., & Terenzini, P. T. (1991). *How college affects students.* San Francisco, CA: Jossey-Bass.

Patton, L. D., & Hannon, M. D. (2008). Collaboration for cultural programming: Engaging culture centers, multicultural affairs, and student activities offices as partners. In S. R. Harper (Ed.), *Creating inclusive campus environments: For cross-cultural learning and student engagement* (pp. 139-154). Washington, DC: National Association of Student Personnel Administrators.

Pauk, W., & Owens, R. J. (2014). *How to study in college* (11th ed.). Boston, MA: Wadsworth.

Peña, E. V. (2014). Marginalization of published scholarship on students with disabilities in higher education journals. *Journal of College Student Development, 55*(1), 30-40.

Peterson-Karlan, G. R. (2011). Technology to support writing by students with learning and academic disabilities: Recent research trends and findings. *Assistive Technology Outcomes and Benefits, 7*(1), 39-62.

Pollak, D. (2009). *Neurodiversity in higher education: Positive responses to specific learning differences.* Malden, MA: Wiley-Blackwell.

Preece, J. E., Roberts, N. L., Beecher, M. E., Rash, P. D., Shwalb, D. A., & Martinelli Jr., E. A. (2007). Academic advisors and students with disabilities: A national survey of advisors' experiences and needs. *NACADA Journal, 27*(2), 57-72.

Price, L., & Patton, J. R. (2003). A new world order: Connecting adult developmental theory to learning disabilities. *Remedial and Special Education, 24*(6), 328-338.

Prince-Hughes, D. (2003, January 3). Understanding college students with autism. *Chronicle of Higher Education,* p. B16. Retrieved from https://www.chronicle.com/article/Understanding-College-Students/3344

Raue, K., & Lewis, L. (2011). *Students with disabilities at degree-granting postsecondary institutions: First look* (NCES 2011–018). U.S. Department of Education, National Center for Education Statistics. Washington, DC: U.S. Government Printing Office.

Rawson, M. B. (1981). A diversity model for dyslexia. In G. Pavlidis & T. Miles (Eds.), *Dyslexia research and its application to education* (pp. 13-34). Chichester, England: Wiley & Sons.

Reddy, Y. M., & Andrade, H. (2010). A review of rubric use in higher education. *Assessment & Evaluation in Higher Education, 35*(4), 435-448.

Richard, M. M. (1995). Pathways to success for the college student with ADD: Accommodations and preferred practices. *Journal of Postsecondary Education and Disability, 11*, 16-30.

Robison, J. E. (2018, April 8). *Be different: A personal story of ASD.* Speech presented at Landmark College, Putney, VT.

Rode, D. L., & Cawthon, T. W. (2010). Theoretical perspectives on orientation. In J. A. Ward-Roof (Ed.), *Designing successful transitions: A guide for orienting students to college* (Monograph No. 13, 3rd ed., pp. 11-28). Columbia, SC: University of South Carolina, National Resource Center for The First-Year Experience and Students in Transition.

Sandin, S., Lichtenstein, P., Kula-Halkola, R., Hultman, C., Larsson, H., & Reichenberg, A. (2017). The heritability of autism spectrum disorder. *JAMA, 318*(12), 1182-1184.

Sarkis, S. M. (2008). Success for the ADHD college student. *The ADHD Report, 16*(5), 1-5.

Schlossberg, N. (1981). A model for analyzing human adaptation to transition. *The Counseling Psychologist, 9*(2), 2-18.

Schneps, M. H., Thomson, J. M., Chen, C., Sonnert, G., & Pomplun, M. (2013). E-readers are more effective than paper for some with dyslexia. *PLoS ONE, 8*(9), 1-9.

Schudde, L. T. (2011). The causal effect of campus residency on college student retention. *The Review of Higher Education, 34*(4), 581-610.

Schulenberg, J. E., Johnston, L. D., O'Malley, P. M., Bachman, J. G., Miech, R. A., & Patrick, M. E. (2017). *Monitoring the future national survey results on drug use, 1975-2016: Volume II, college students and adults ages 19-55.* Ann Arbor, MI: Institute for Social Research, The University of Michigan. Retrieved from http://www.monitoringthefuture.org/pubs/monographs/mtf-vol2_2016.pdf

Scott, S., Shaw, S., & McGuire, J. (in press). Universal design for instruction: A new paradigm for adult instruction in postsecondary education. *Remedial and Special Education.* Retrieved from http://www.facultyware.uconn.edu/UDI_principles.htm

Sessa, V. I., Alonso, N., Farago, P., Schettino, G., Tacchi, K., & Bragger, J. D. (2017). Student organizations as avenues for leader learning and development. In D. M. Rosch (Ed.), *The role of student organizations in developing leadership* (New Directions for Student Leadership, No. 155, pp. 21-32). San Francisco, CA: Jossey-Bass.

Sharma, M. C. (n.d.). *Lesson plan.* Retrieved from http://www.dyscalculia.org/experts/sharma-s-ctlm/sharma-lesson-planning

Shaw, S. F. (2012). Disability documentation: Using all the data. *Journal of Postsecondary Education and Disability, 25*, 277-282.

Shaw, S. F., & Dukes, L. L. (2013). Transition to postsecondary education: A call for evidence-based practice. *Career Development and Transition for Exceptional Individuals, 36*(1), 51-57.

Shaw, S. F., Keenan, W. R., Madaus, J. W., & Banerjee, M. (2010). Disability documentation, the Americans With Disabilities Act Amendments Act and the summary of performance: How are they linked? *Journal of Postsecondary Education and Disability, 22*, 142-150.

Shaywitz, S. (2013, May). *Defining my dyslexia.* Retrieved from http://dyslexia.yale.edu/defining-my-dyslexia/

Shea, L., & Donahue, A. (2017, October). *Lessons learned: Improving the college transition for college students with ASD.* Presentation at the National Conference on Students in Transition, Costa Mesa, CA.

Shifrer, D., Muller, C., & Callahan, R. (2011). Disproportionality and learning disabilities: Parsing apart race, socioeconomic status, and language. *Journal of Learning Disabilities, 44*(3), 246-257. https://doi.org/10.1177/0022219410374236

Shmulsky, S., & Gobbo, K. (2013). Autism spectrum in the college classroom: Strategies for instructors. *Community College Journal of Research and Practice, 37*(6), 490-495.

Shoham, R., Sonuga-Barke, E., Aloni, H., Yaniv, I., & Pollak, Y. (2016). ADHD-associated risk taking is linked to exaggerated views of the benefits of positive outcomes. *Scientific Reports, 6*, 34833. https://doi.org/10.1038/srep34833

Showers, A. H., & Kinsman, J. W. (2017). Factors that contribute to college success for students with learning disabilities. *Learning Disability Quarterly, 40*(2), 81-90.

Sniatecki, J. L., Perry, H. B., & Snell, L. H. (2015). Faculty attitudes and knowledge regarding college students with disabilities. *Journal of Postsecondary Education and Disability, 28*(3), 259-275.

Soares, N., & Patel, D. (2015). Dyscalculia. *International Journal of Child and Adolescent Health, 8*(1), 15-26.

Sparks, R. L., & Lovett, B. J. (2009). College students with learning disability diagnoses: Who are they and how do they perform? *Journal of Learning Disabilities, 42*(6), 494-510.

Starcke, K., Wiesen, C., Trotzke, P., & Brand, M. (2016). Effects of acute laboratory stress on executive functions. *Frontiers in Psychology, 31*(7), 1-8.

Stodden, R. A., Brown, S. E., & Roberts, K. (2011). Disability-friendly university environments: Conducting a climate assessment. *New Directions for Higher Education, 154*, 83-92.

Stout, A., & Schwartz, A. (2014). "It'll grow organically and naturally": The reciprocal relationship between student groups and disability studies on college campuses. *Disability Studies Quarterly, 34*(2).

Sullivan, A., & Caterino, L. C. (2008). Addressing the sexuality and sex education of individuals with autism spectrum disorders. *Education and Treatment of Children, 31*(3), 381-394.

Swanson, J., Castellanos, F. X., Murias, M., LaHoste, G., & Kennedy, J. (1998). Cognitive neuroscience of attention deficit hyperactivity disorder and hyperkinetic disorder. *Current Opinion in Neurobiology, 8*(2), 263-271.

Sweller, J. (2010). Element interactivity and intrinsic, extraneous, and germane cognitive load. *Educational Psychology Review, 22*(2), 123-138.

Taymans, J. M., Swanson, H. L., Schwarz, R. L., Gregg, N., Hack, M., & Gerber, P. J. (2009). *Learning to achieve: A review of the research literature on serving adults with learning disabilities.* Retrieved from https://lincs.ed.gov/publications/pdf/L2ALiteratureReview09.pdf

Tinto, V. (1975). Dropout from higher education: A theoretical synthesis of recent research. *Review of Educational Research, 45,* 89-125.

Tinto, V. (2007). Research and practice of student retention: What next? *Journal of College Student Retention: Research, Theory & Practice, 8*(1), 1-19.

Tjaden, P. G., & Thoennes, N. (1998). *Stalking in America: Findings from the national violence against women survey.* Retrieved from https://www.ncjrs.gov/pdffiles/169592.pdf

Tobolowsky, B. F. (2008). Sophomores in transition: The forgotten year. *New Directions for Higher Education, 144,* 59-67.

Troiano, P. F., Liefeld, J. A., & Trachtenberg, J. V. (2010). Academic support and college success for postsecondary students with learning disabilities. *Journal of College Reading and Learning, 40*(2), 35-44.

Uccula, A., Enna, M., & Mulatti, C. (2014). Colors, colored overlays, and reading skills. *Frontiers in Psychology, 5*(833), 1-4.

U. S. Department of Labor. (2014). *Economic picture of the disability community project.* Retrieved from https://www.dol.gov/odep/topics/DisabilityEmploymentStatistics.htm

U. S. Equal Employment Opportunity Commission. (n.d.). *Americans with Disabilities Act of 1990 (ADA) charges (Charges filed with EEOC) (includes concurrent charges with Title VII, ADEA, EPA, and GINA) FY 1997-FY 2017.* Retrieved from https://www.eeoc.gov/eeoc/statistics/enforcement/ada-charges.cfm

U. S. Government Accountability Office. (2010). *Students with disabilities: More information and guidance could improve opportunities in physical education and athletics.* (GAO Publication No. GAO-10-519). Retrieved from: https://www.gao.gov/assets/310/305775.html

UDI Online Project. (2010). *Students with disabilities and online learning* (Technical Brief # 04). Storrs, CT: University of Connecticut, Center on Postsecondary Education and Disability. Retrieved from http://www.udi.uconn.edu/index.php?q=content/technical-brief-students-disabilities-and-online-learning

VanHees, V., Moyson, T., & Roeyers, H. (2014). Higher education experiences of students with autism spectrum disorder: Challenges, benefits and support needs. *Journal of Autism and Developmental Disorders, 45*(6), 1673-1688.

Van Rheenen, D., Grigorieff, M., & Adams, J. N. (2017). Envisioning innovation at the intersection of sport and disability: A blueprint for American higher education. *Journal of Higher Education Athletics & Innovation, 1*(2), 92-109.

Virtue, E. E., Wells, G., & Virtue, A. D. (2017). Supporting sophomore success through a new learning community model. *Learning Communities Research and Practice, 5*(2), Article 6. Retrieved from https://washingtoncenter.evergreen.edu/lcrpjournal/vol5/iss2/6

Vogel, S. A., Holt, J. K., Sligar, S., & Leake, E. (2008). Assessment of campus climate to enhance student success. *Journal of Postsecondary Education and Disability, 21*(1), 15-31.

Webber, K. L., Krylow, R. B., & Zhang, Q. (2013). Does involvement really matter? Indicators of college student success and satisfaction. *Journal of College Student Development, 54*(6), 591-611.

Wehmeyer, M. L. (1992). Self-determination and the education of students with mental retardation. *Education and Training of the Mentally Retarded, 27*, 302-314.

Weisbuch, R., & Cassuto, L. (2016). *Reforming doctoral education, 1990 to 2015: Recent initiatives and future prospects.* Retrieved from https://mellon.org/media/filer_public/35/32/3532f16c-20c4-4213-805d-356f85251a98/report-on-doctoral-education-reform_june-2016.pdf

West, S. L., Graham, C. W., & Temple, P. (2017). Rates and correlates of binge drinking among college students with disabilities, United States, 2013. *Public Health Reports, 132*(4), 496-504.

Wheeler, M. (n.d.). *Academic supports for college students with an autism spectrum disorder: An overview.* Retrieved from https://www.iidc.indiana.edu/pages/Academic-Supports-for-College-Students-with-an-Autism-Spectrum-Disorder

Wilens, T. E. (2004). Attention-deficit/hyperactivity disorder and the substance use disorders: The nature of the relationship, subtypes at risk, and treatment issues. *Psychiatric Clinics, 27*(2), 283-301.

Williams, L. B. (2016). Student life on the autism spectrum: Helping to build a more inclusive campus. *Change: The Magazine of Higher Learning, 48*(4), 48-54.

Williams, L. B. (2018, February 8). The nexus of autism and Title IX. *Inside Higher Ed.* Retrieved from https://www.insidehighered.com

Wilson, A. (n.d.). *What is happening in the brain?* Retrieved from http://www.aboutdyscalculia.org/causes.html

Wilus, M. (2013). Coaching strategies for exceptional (ADHD) athletes. *Graduate Annual, 1*(1), 36-40.

World Health Organization (WHO). (2018). *Disabilities.* Retrieved from http://www.who.int/topics/disabilities/en/

Young, D. A., Schreiner, L. A., & McIntosh, E. J. (2015). *Investigating sophomore student success: The National Survey of Sophomore-Year Initiatives and the Sophomore Experiences Survey, 2014* (Research Reports on College Transitions, No. 6). Columbia, SC: University of South Carolina, National Resource Center for The First-Year Experience and Students in Transition.

Zubal-Ruggieri, R. (2016, November). *Academic programs in disability studies.* Retrieved from http://disabilitystudies.syr.edu/programs-list/

INDEX

NOTE: Page numbers with italicized *f* or *t* indicate figures or tables respectively.

A

ableism, definition of, 6

ableist model. *See also* social justice or ableist model

abstract thinking, students with ASD and, 62

academic programs, advisors and accommodations for, 75–76

academic support services, 74–75

acceptance, of disability identity, 33

access, use of term, 92

accessibility

    of course content, universal design and, 69

    of digital tools, 68*f*

accessibility office. *See also* campus disability services; disability support services

    student contact with, 10

accommodations. *See also* Americans with Disabilities Act; classroom supports; disability identity; Rehabilitation Act, Section 504

    digital texts and exams and, 50

    faculty training and, 92

    for leadership activities, 87

    legal basis for, 10

    letter, campus disability services and, 28

    process, 34–36, 47

    for students with ASD, 62, 95–96

    transition process and, 8–9

accommodations model, 5, 56, 100

action, in Brown's ADD/ADHD model, 58*f*, 59*t*

activation, in Brown's ADD/ADHD model, 58*f*, 59*t*

activist activities, students with disabilities and, 83

ADA. See Americans with Disabilities Act

ADA coordinator. *See also* disability support services

    advisor referrals to, 75

Adams, J. N., 85

Adderall, 80

ADHD, students with. *See also* attention-deficit/hyperactivity disorder; executive function

    assessment, 22

    asynchronous online courses and, 67

    athletics, club sports, and intramurals and, 85

    campus activities and events and, 84

    classroom supports for students with, 55–56

    coaching services for, 98–99

    college transition for, 37

    employment search and, 45

    leadership challenges for, 86–87

    medication issues for, 22, 77–78

    personal care and, 79–80

    profiles of, 20–25

    relationships and sexuality, 78–79

    signs of, 23–25, 23*f*

    substance abuse and, 25, 37, 80

    text-to-speech (TTS) readers and, 50

About the Authors

Linda Hecker is a founding faculty member of Landmark College who retired in July 2017 and was recently appointed professor emeritus. She served in multiple roles: directing tutorial and teacher training programs; teaching English, study skills, and music classes; and as an academic advisor and dean. She was appointed to the Landmark College Institute for Research and Training in 2001, where she led professional learning initiatives for educators around the world. She frequently presents workshops, seminars, and graduate courses on topics related to learning differences and has delivered seminars for the Foreign Service Department's language instructors. Hecker is the author of numerous articles and book chapters, including work on multisensory learning and supportive technology. She received her BA from Brandeis University and her M.Ed from the University of Hartford.

Adam R. Lalor is lead education specialist with the Landmark College Institute for Research and Training. His research interests include postsecondary transition for students with disabilities and the preparation of faculty and staff members to serve the needs of students with disabilities. With more than a decade of experience in higher education administration, Lalor has worked in academic support services, admission, athletics, residential life, and sexual violence prevention and education. He regularly presents at conferences, institutions of higher education, and high schools around the nation, and currently serves as co-chair of the Learning Disabilities Association of America's Research Committee. Lalor holds a doctorate in educational psychology from the University of Connecticut's Neag School of Education, with a focus on postsecondary transition.

Lynne C. Shea is currently the dean of Liberal Studies and the Arts at Landmark College and a professor of literature. Previously, she was the executive director of the Landmark College Institute for Research and Training and has served in a number of other faculty and administrative roles, including as director of several U.S. Department of Education-funded projects. Shea was the editor of *The Landmark College Guides to Instruction for Students with Learning Disabilities*, and her interests include self-advocacy for students with learning differences and teaching Shakespeare and African American literature. She has a BA in English from Dartmouth College and an MA in English from Middlebury College.